D0193510

An Adult Child's Guide To What Is "Normal"

John C. Friel, Ph.D.
Linda D. Friel, M.A., C.C.D.P.

Health Communications, Inc.
Deerfield Beach, Florida

John C. Friel, Ph.D.
Linda D. Friel, M.A.
Friel & Associates/Lifeworks
St. Paul, Minnesota

Library of Congress Cataloging-in-Publication Date
Friel, John C.
  An Adult Child's Guide to what is "normal." John C. Friel,
Linda D. Friel.
      p.   c.m.
  Includes bibliographical references.
  ISBN 1-55874-090-2
  1. Adult children of alcoholics — Rehabilitation. 2. Adult chil-
dren of narcotic addicts — Rehabilitation. 3. Adult children of
dysfunctional families — Rehabilitation. I. Friel, Linda D. II. Title.
III. Title: Dysfunctional families.
HV5132.F753   1990   90-4754
362.29' 13—dc20   CIP

ISBN 1-55874-090-2

Publisher: Health Communications, Inc.
            3201 S.W. 15th Street
            Deerfield Beach, FL 33442-8190

Cover design by Graphic Expressions

Dedication

This book is dedicated to our children, Kristin, Rebecca and David, whose lives and growth and healing make us feel eternally grateful; and to the hundreds of clients, workshop participants and letter-writers who have shared their recoveries with us and who have thanked us for our work.

Acknowledgments

We would like to thank all of the professionals, clients and friends who have touched our lives over the years, as they shared their pain and joy with us and allowed us to share our pain and joy with them. Special thanks to Gary Seidler, Peter Vegso, Michael Miller, Luann Jarvie, Suzanne Smith, Reta Thomas, Edith Conner and Marie Stilkind for their support and encouragement of our work, help with our manuscript and for being there when we needed them. Health Communications and U.S. Journal Training, Inc., have reached a lot of folks out there over the years.

Other Books By Authors

Adult Children
The Secrets of Dysfunctional Families

Pamphlets

Life On My Own Terms

Co-dependency And Family Rules
with Robert Subby

Co-dependency And The Search For Identity
with Robert Subby

About The Authors

John C. Friel, Ph.D., is a psychologist in private practice in St. Paul, Minnesota; director of the St. Paul/Minneapolis Lifeworks Clinic, an intensive, short-term treatment program for Adult Child, Co-dependency, Addiction and Compulsivity issues; and adjunct associate professor of psychology at St. Mary's College Graduate Center in Minneapolis. Dr. Friel earned his B.A. in psychology from the University of San Francisco in 1969, and his Ph.D. in psychology from West Virginia University in 1976. He is a nationally recognized author, trainer, speaker and consultant in the areas of dysfunctional family systems, co-dependency, adult child issues, stress and addictions. A native of Marin County, California, Dr. Friel has lived in Minnesota since 1973.

Linda D. Friel, M.A., C.C.D.P., is a psychologist in private practice, a therapist and trainer for the Lifeworks Clinic, and she designed and implemented one of the first hospital-based co-dependency treatment programs in the U.S. She specializes in psychotherapy for Adult Children, Co-dependency and Survivors of Physical and Sexual Abuse; and is also a nationally recognized author, trainer and consultant in the areas of dysfunctional families, co-dependency, adult child issues and addictions. A native of Minneapolis, Minnesota, Linda earned her B.A. from Mankato State University in 1971, taught special education classes for eight years and earned her M.A. in counseling and psychological services from St. Mary's College in Minnesota in 1980.

The Friels have consulted with a wide range of hospitals, treatment centers, colleges, universities, corporations, small businesses, medical practices, law firms, nursing associations and government agencies in Minnesota, the rest of the United States and Canada.

Preface

This book takes off where our first book ended. In *Adult Children: The Secrets Of Dysfunctional Families* (Friel & Friel, 1988), we presented in depth the forces and themes and causes of family dysfunction and co-dependency. At the end of that book, we talked about recovery and what we can look forward to if we take the very big risk of trying to heal.

As we continue our own recoveries and watch the recoveries of the many courageous clients with whom we work, we notice that there is a big gap in the literature . . . that people get to a point where they have done a lot of scary work about their childhood traumas and have healed a lot, but then don't know where to go from there. People say, "Okay, I've done this early childhood work, but now what? I've worked through this dysfunction, but what is *functional?*" Janet Woititz perhaps stated it best when she said that adult children don't know what "normal" is (Woititz, 1983).

We assume that what Woititz was implying by her elegant statement is that we adult children and co-dependents don't know what "healthy and functional" are. What is statistically normal, as we showed in our first book, is not necessarily healthy or functional. Sometimes it is, and sometimes not. We believe that the human race, like each individual human being, is on an evolutionary path of gradual improvement; and that each of us is trying to unfold toward greater actualization, dignity, compassion and love.

It is the same with cultures. In ancient Greece and Rome it was accepted practice to kill infants, especially female ones, but we no longer accept this as part of our culture. It was once statistically "normal" to beat children with sticks, boards, belts and whips but we now see this as child abuse. It was once the norm (and perhaps still is, but won't be forever) to look the other way, bury our heads in the sand and pretend that the sexual abuse of children was either okay or didn't exist very much. While we have become a much more humane, compassionate society in some ways, we are still evolving and improving. At least we hope so.

And so we have written this book to serve as a guide and, yes, even a "how to," for people who have already done a good chunk of family-of-origin and feelings work around the overt and covert abuse that happened to them as children. This is a book about *how to be more functional* and *healthy*. It is a book for those of us who have done two years of work, have our major addiction in the healing mode, and who are now wondering where on earth we're going to learn all those healthy things that our parents couldn't teach us because they didn't know either.

We caution everyone reading this book to choose what works for you and to ignore what doesn't. We also caution you to *hold yourself accountable* when things in your life don't work out. Some of the advice in this book may not be for you. But if you find yourself not being able to follow through with healthy changes in your own life in the here and now, please get back into therapy and work through some more of your deeper issues.

Realize that there are some universal principles of healthy living, but that the specifics have to be molded to fit your own style of life. Realize, too, that if there are several healthy options for you and if you can't get *any* of them to work, you may need to go back to the drawing board and heal some more. Finally, realize that this is *always* the way it works. There is nothing to be horribly ashamed of if you have to go back and dig a little deeper. We *all* have to do this at various times in our lives.

Despite our own human limitations and frailties as therapists and authors, we will try to present here what we and many professionals view to be *functional and healthy* responses to the many challenges, problems and traps that face each of us on a daily basis. We wish you well on your journey to recovery. We hope this book can help you in that journey in one or two little ways.

John C. Friel, Ph.D.
Licensed Consulting Psychologist

Linda D. Friel, M.A., C.C.D.P.
Licensed Psychologist

St. Paul, Minnesota

Contents

PART I

The Road
To Being
Functional

Children naturally want to be like their parents, and
to do what they do.

William Cobbett
Advice To Young Men, V, 1829

1

65 Characteristics Of Adult Children Becoming Functional People

Based on the comments and letters we have received over the past two years about our first book, one of the most powerful things we wrote was the list of 65 characteristics of adult children from dysfunctional families. In that list, we tried to show phenomenologically that our dysfunction always occurs in the extremes; that the great tragedy for many of us is that in our sincere attempts to make *our* lives better than they were in childhood, we go to the other extreme and create equally painful dysfunction. To provide some balance to our first book and our first list, we present here a complementary list which applies to . . .

Adult Children Becoming Functional People . . .

1. We are people who hit age 28 or 39 or 47 and suddenly find something is wrong that we can no longer fix by ourselves. Then we make a choice to get into recovery, seek help, do a lot of painful work and then live happy lives.

2. We are people who gaze at our peers on the street or at a party and say to ourselves, "It's nice to know that I'm not alone in the world."

3. Or we say, "It's comforting to know that there are several people in the world who know who I really am and accept me for that."

4. We are people who love our spouses or partners, care deeply for our children and find ourselves growing happier and more comfortably in love with them every day.

5. We know that our loved ones will never be perfect, but because we are in recovery, they have permission to get into recovery when they are ready.

6. We take risks in our careers when it makes sense and move into something new when we need to.

7. We are *recovering* chemical dependents, sexual dependents and eating disordered.

8. We are *recovering* migraine sufferers, exercise bulimics and work addicts.

9. We have solid friendships whether we are extroverted or introverted.

10. Some of us grew up in chaotic families and were weaned on alcoholism, incest and physical, emotional and spiritual abuse. And now we are healing from those wounds.

11. Some of us were especially paralyzed because the dysfunction we experienced was so subtle (covert) that we couldn't even begin to put a finger on what it was that happened to us. But through a lot of hard work, we *did* put a finger on that covert abuse. Now we are noticing it when it happens to us in our daily lives, and we set boundaries around it.

12. Some of us were compared to a brother or sister who did well in school, but we have gone on now to find the worth and value that *we* have in life.

13. Others were led to believe that we could only have worth and value if we became plumbers or doctors, electricians, lawyers or psychologists. Now we know that this isn't true for *anyone*.

14. Some walked on eggshells throughout childhood because the family was poor. Dad worked two jobs, Mom raised

five kids pretty much by herself and everyone was tired and on edge most of the time. Now in our recoveries, regardless of our wealth or finances, we have serenity and spirituality, and we make choices that help us to reduce stress.

15. Many of us were emotionally neglected because no one was physically there for us; or because they were there for us with material things but were absent emotionally. In our lives today, we know that material things are important for our survival and that emotional nurturing is as important as physical nurturing.

16. Some of us were spoiled and smothered out of misguided love; seduced to stay in the nest years after our friends had gone out into the world and begun their adult lives. We have finally cut the cord even though it was painful, and we now welcome the responsibilities and rights that come with growing up.

17. Many of us were once afraid of people, especially authority figures. Now we act with self-respect and other-respect regardless of one's station in life.

18. Others of us used to frighten people, especially our loved ones, but now we have made amends for those offenses and find other ways to meet our needs without bullying our loved ones.

19. We are people who accept others for their beliefs, rather than fearing or hating them as we used to do.

20. We used to let others use and abuse us, or we used to use and abuse others; but we don't do that much anymore.

21. We are people who used to have only anger, sadness, fear or smiles. We find today that we have a whole range of emotions that are appropriate for the situation.

22. We used to try so hard that we lost or try so little that we never lived life at all. Now we know when to try and when to back off, and we keep those efforts in balance.

23. We are men and women who no longer have to look "picture perfect," because we have shared ourselves with others, and we know that no one is perfect. What's inside of us is much more consistent with what's on the outside now.

24. When we hit skid row, we felt like we finally belonged somewhere. Now we know that where we belong is with other recovering people.
25. We used to have lots of depression and rage. Now we have more healthy sadness and healthy anger.
26. We used to think ourselves into emptiness or feel ourselves into chaos. Now we keep a balance between what we think, feel and do.
27. We used to be on emotional roller-coasters or in emotional vacuums. Today we have feelings that fit the situation, and we know what to do when we get bogged down in those feelings or when we are stuck and can't feel them.
28. Instead of smiling while we slam the kitchen cabinet shut because we're really angry, or slamming the cabinet angrily when we're really sad, we avoid being passive-aggressive and ashamed of our sadness and have surrounded ourselves with others who also operate in functional ways. We now talk it out.
29. Instead of abusing ourselves and taking care of others, we now take care of our own needs in healthy ways and care without bondage about the other human beings in our lives.
30. When we are unhappy now, instead of being afraid to tell anyone for fear of being "found out," we know who it is safe to talk to and we talk to them about our unhappiness.
31. We still have trouble relating to our sons, our daughters or both, because parent-child relationships can be hard at times; but we know how to get out of the trouble and communicate with our children; and they feel safe communicating with us.
32. Now we can make love with our partner when both of us choose to and know how to get emotionally close to our partner as a prerequisite to sex.
33. We still look to others who are wiser than us for guidance but we aren't enslaved by what others do. We know we can make our own way in life and it doesn't have to match everyone else's life.

34. Instead of feeling better or worse than others, we feel as if we belong somewhere and it feels great.
35. We get stuck in our lives sometimes, but now we know how to get unstuck.
36. We are at peace with our pasts, look forward to the challenges of the future and enjoy the moment.
37. We don't work ourselves to death. We work hard, but we also know how to enjoy being still, quiet, playful and relaxed.
38. We are satisfied.
39. God is neither to be feared nor expected to do it all for us. Our concept of Higher Power fits for us, we are comfortable with our spirituality and we know that we have to do a lot of the work ourselves.
40. We appreciate people who are different and see how they enrich our lives.
41. We can get out of friendships that aren't working for us anymore; and we can do so with respect to both ourselves and the other person.
42. We no longer get hooked on things in ways that hurt us.
43. We deal with our inner conflicts ourselves now. We own them and hold ourselves accountable for them, so that we no longer have to project them onto our children.
44. We are proud of our bodies, warts and all.
45. We know why we are here, and we ask for continued guidance so that we can continue to know.
46. We know that suffering is part of life, but that the kind of chronic suffering we experienced because of the abuses that happened to us in childhood does not have to continue.
47. Now we see a police car and just keep driving. Unless of course, we are speeding and the police officer wants us to pull over.
48. We now know that, while security is important, false security is not as important as our own dignity and worth.
49. Instead of demanding love and rarely getting it, we love ourselves now, have good friends and accept love as a gift when it comes into our lives. We give love freely when it makes sense to do so.

50. Instead of wishing for things and never getting them, we now ask for what we need and want, knowing that we will not always get it, but continuing to try where our chances are optimal.

51. We have hope, we rarely get pessimistic and we live life as it comes.

52. We can eat in a restaurant alone and be comfortable. In fact, our alone time is very important to us.

53. When we have a problem or a complaint, we know how to assert ourselves without being rageful or passive-aggressive.

54. When we fall in love, we stay in the relationship long enough to find out if it is a fit for us. If we stay, we can keep our own identities while still loving the other person.

55. We neither smother nor crush those we love. We care for them without hovering and without trying to control them all the time.

56. Some of us will turn the tide of history by our actions, and some of us will live in obscurity, but all of us will have great worth and value in our lives and can be comfortable with both those less powerful and more powerful than we are.

57. Rather than fantasizing about how perfect our parents were or ragefully hating them indefinitely, we will do recovery work that lets us be at peace with them, even if they are still abusive and we have to keep our distance from them.

58. Our guilt about how we were treated compared to a siblings and our jealousy about how they were treated compared to us will be worked through in therapy and laid to rest. We won't deny our pasts but we won't be slaves to our pasts either.

59. We will stop hating and overprotecting our parents. They will become "de-mythologized," and our feelings about them will be based in reality.

60. If we were sexually abused, we no longer blame ourselves. We know that children have no power over adults and that sexual abuse is always the fault of the perpetrator.

61. We have grieved the fact that we had a parent who was chronically ill when we were growing up.
62. We have grieved the fact that we had a parent who was mentally ill when we were growing up.
63. We have grieved and dealt with the fear of abandonment stemming from the fact that we had no parents when we were growing up.
64. Instead of just surviving, we are beginning to celebrate our lives each day.
65. We are lovers of life whose Little Child has been set free!

Regardless of why we were adult children from dysfunctional families, we are now Adult Children Becoming Functional People because . . .

Something happened to us a long time ago. It happened more than once. It hurt us. We protected ourselves the only way we knew how. We have begun to remove our veils of denial and to learn new ways of living and feeling and sharing and being. Our lives are starting to work now, and we feel whole.

2

How To Use This Book

Being Functional

It may feel scary at first. There may be lots of guilt. It may be hard at first to separate the healthy guilt from the co-dependent guilt. There may be loneliness because facing temporary loneliness is the key to avoiding the traps of our dysfunctional pasts. There may be fear because change *always* produces some fear. As you read through this book, you might even want to skim it in the beginning. Look at the chapter titles. See what it's about. Then read it from beginning to end, perhaps marking the chapters or issues that are most on your mind these days. Then you can use it as a trouble-shooting guide . . . as *one possible road-map* when you find yourself struggling with a particular part of your life.

Having trouble with what to do for the holidays? Flip to that chapter, read it through and let the suggestions there *open your mind* to some new possibilities. If the only thing this book does for you is open your mind to new possibilities that you come up with on your own, then we have succeeded in our goal.

Much of this book grew out of a series of workshops that we do entitled, "Co-Dependency Traps: Getting Hooked And Unhooked." The Traps we get into are the result of our dysfunctional pasts. In fact, the Traps we get into are *re-enactments* of patterns from our childhoods. This means that as we were growing up in our families, each of us was exposed to certain rules about living, getting our needs met and interacting with each other. We learned about men from the men in our families. We learned about women from the women in our families. And we learned about ourselves from the way we were treated in our families.

If we were ignored, we will grow up to ignore ourselves and our needs as adults. If we were hurt, we will hurt ourselves as adults. If we were physically or emotionally seduced as children, we will grow up and become either seducers or victims or both.

We *re-enact and repeat the patterns* of living that were formed for us when we were children. We emphasize *patterns* here because this is the biggest Trap of all for so many of us. I look at the *specific details* of my adult life and say to myself, "My life is much healthier than Dad's. Dad was an alcoholic, but I don't drink at all!"

But often the *pattern* is the same. While I may not drink at all, I may work compulsively, exercise compulsively or avoid intimacy by watching too much television. I may be critical, perfectionistic and terrified of having my feelings, just like Dad was. But because I don't drink at all, I *believe* that my life is very different from Dad's even though I have re-enacted my family of origin right down to the last detail except the drinking. Keep this principle in mind as you read this book.

For all intents and purposes, a good portion of this book is simply a "cookbook" of various normal life problems and how to deal with them in a *functional* way. It's really pretty simple. It is based on years and even lifetimes of experiences from our friends, our colleagues, our clients and ourselves. After all, even cooks use cookbooks now and then. We have tried to compile some of the more common Traps that catch us in various areas of our lives; and we have tried to group them into categories that make some logical or emotional sense. In many cases, there is a lot of overlap between categories. Setting boundaries with a friend is going to be similar to setting boundaries with a partner or boss or child. But there are differences, too. Many of us find it easier to say "no" to a door-to-door salesperson than to our spouse. So we invite you to be flexible in using this book. If our discussion of one situation fits well for another situation in your life, then by all means apply it there. Part I of this book includes a brief review of pertinent material from *Adult Children: The Secrets Of Dysfunctional Families* (Friel & Friel, 1988), so that the reader has a base from which to work. It also includes new material on recovery and some pointers on what recovery looks like and how it feels.

The rest of the book deals with common life situations and how to be more **functional**. By no means can we cover all of life's problems, nor can we cover all the possible healthy ways to handle those problems. We hope our examples can be guides, that they can stimulate you to think of your own unique solutions and that they can give you a *feel* for what can be done to take care of yourself in respectful ways. Some of the short chapters state very specific problems and traps and suggest clear, direct solutions. Others are simply lists, stories or bits of wisdom that we have gleaned from our clinical work over the years. Take what makes sense to you and leave the rest for someone else, just as you might do if attending a healthy 12-Step meeting.

Above all, remember that . . .

1. Recovery is a process.
2. We don't have to do it perfectly, even *in* recovery.
3. Until we have done a good bit of our core family-of-origin work, the practical solutions offered in this book will most likely backfire.

In other words, begin to enjoy the relief that comes from accepting the truth that we are never recover*ed*.

Paradoxically, when we stop trying to recover perfectly, we find that our growth and health move along quite nicely. When we beat ourselves up for "not doing it right," we take one step backwards. If you find that trying out our suggestions always seems to backfire, then it probably means you have another piece of therapy work to do around your family of origin. In that case, go ahead and have your anger and shame about having to get back into therapy, and then get back into therapy for awhile until you've worked it through.

Last of all, take some of the wisdom offered by so many successful business people: *There is no such thing as failure.*

When a successful person gets into a business venture that goes "belly up," he or she says, "Oh, I can see that *that* doesn't work for *me*. What have I learned from this experience? And what shall I try next?" When we aren't working our recovery program, we say, "I am a failure. Why try anymore?"

Life will always have its ups and downs. Until we work through our core guilt, shame and fear issues, we will be at the mercy of life's "downs." We must emphasize that the successful person said, "I failed, but *I am not a failure*," while the person who gives up on life altogether says, "*I am a failure*."

It is very important for those of us who are in recovery to share our failures with others who will say, "Yes, I can see that it didn't work out for you," and who by their actions and their words say, "And I care about you and will still be here." *That* is how unhealthy shame and fear go away.

If trying out the suggestions in this book always backfires, see that information about yourself as a *gift*. It is important information. It is neither good nor bad. It is a sign, telling you where to go next. Until we are able to make friends with our failure, we will continue to be enslaved by it.

Above all, remember that each of us has certain *vulnerabilities*, and these may differ from person to person. Joe might be a "sucker" for a pretty face and a charming smile, while Bob might be a "sucker" for false praise from co-workers. Sue might have problems with being alone, while Kathy might find it difficult to be with people.

While we as human beings share a lot in common, we are also unique. Each of us must discover our own strengths and weaknesses. Each of us must find our own traps and hooks and disarm them. No one can do it for us, and no two of us will do it exactly the same way. Recovery requires intimacy with self, above all.

3

From Shame And Blame
To Respect And
Healthy Love

Alcoholic. Co-Dependent. Adult Child. Dysfunctional Family System. Sexually Addicted. Eating Disordered. Compulsive. Relationship Addicted. Enmeshed. Lonely. Depressed. Can't Feel. Burnout.

You name it. We've said it before and we'll say it again. While many of these are primary diseases, beneath the disease they are also about our *feelings* and our *intimacy*. They're about what we *didn't* get as children.

Some of these problems also can have a very strong genetic, biological component to them and because of that we recommend that you have a thorough physical examination and take a good look at your nutrition before ruling out these possibilities.

For example, if your depression escalates during the winter months, you may be suffering from Seasonal Affective Disorder (SAD) and could profit from being in front of some full-spectrum lights each day. If you try the full-spectrum lights for a few months and still feel depressed, then think about looking a little deeper into your Co-Dependency/Adult Child issues.

Or you may have an imbalanced diet with too much sugar and not enough vitamins and protein. If so, change your diet for a few months and see if things improve. If it's hard to get off the sugar, you may be addicted and if you're addicted to sugar, you will need to get into a recovery program.

In *Adult Children: The Secrets Of Dysfunctional Families* (Friel & Friel, 1988), we presented our general model of co-dependency and adult child issues as a way for us and our clients to make some sense out of the continuing merger of mental health and chemical dependency theory. The model is simple and we believe it is powerful because of that. It shows that our diseases are the first to be discovered, our co-dependency is right below the surface, and our core issues of guilt, shame and fear of abandonment exist deeply beneath. This *"Iceberg Model" Of Co-dependency/Adult Child Issues* is shown in Figure 3.1. It means that as adults we have some painful problems which can be best summarized as *identity* and *intimacy* issues; which in turn developed from unmet developmental needs around guilt, shame and fear of abandonment. The core of this model is based on the timeless work of Erik Erikson (1963, 1968).

In *Adult Children* we also presented our definition of co-dependency:

> Co-dependency is a dysfunctional pattern of living which emerges from our family of origin as well as our culture, producing arrested identity development, and resulting in an over-reaction to things outside of us and an under-reaction to things inside of us. Left untreated, it can deteriorate into an addiction.

Whether we are truly "Co-dependent" or just "Have Some Co-dependent Behaviors" will depend on how much Guilt, Shame and Fear of Abandonment we carry into adulthood as baggage from childhood.

We are either clear about who we are or we aren't. Our lives feel good most of the time or they don't. Our arguments and fights either get settled within a few minutes, hours or days (depending on the depth of the issue) or they don't. We can either help our children grow up without unduly controlling and manipulating them or we can't. We either like who we live with, play with and work with or we don't. Then we can do something to change it.

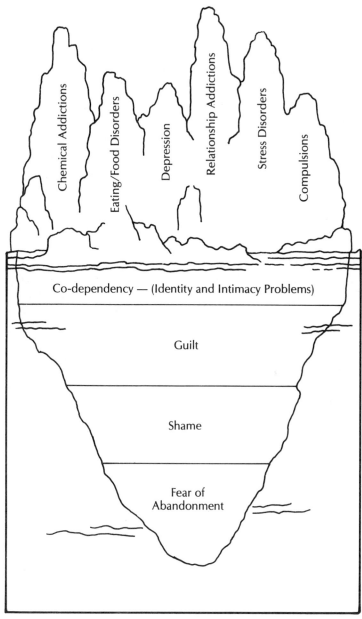

Chemical Addictions

Eating/Food Disorders

Depression

Relationship Addictions

Stress Disorders

Compulsions

Co-dependency — (Identity and Intimacy Problems)

Guilt

Shame

Fear of
Abandonment

©1984 Friel & Friel

**Figure 3.1. Unifying Model Of
Co-dependency and Addictions**

Granted, it would be easy to look at the paragraph above and cry "foul!" "Black and white! Black and white! You're making it all black and white!" But we don't mean to say it's all black and white. What we mean to say is this: Living in the world has its ups and downs. Emotional health means that we have a good share of "ups," that as all human beings we have our share of "downs," and that as healthy human beings we can eventually do something to change the "really-bad-downs-that-keep-happening-over-and-over."

Our Iceberg Model in Figure 3.1 is actually pretty painful to look at and absorb. As therapists, it was hard for us to admit that we had fear which kept us from feeling basically safe in the world; that we had shame which kept us from having dignity and that we had unhealthy guilt which kept us from getting "unstuck." And when those issues develop enough power to begin to over-whelm us today, it is *still* hard to admit that they're there. But we're human, and we get to have our share of "downs," too. We have to struggle with it. We have to admit that it's become unmanageable. We have to share the struggle with our support system. We have to stop and listen to the Little Child inside of us. We have to make friends with our fear instead of pushing it away. We have to stop long enough to listen to what the other person is *feeling* instead of what they're saying. *Most of all, we have to listen to our own feelings.* And month by month and year by year the "ups" get softer and quieter and deeper, and the "downs" get more brief, more enlightening and more respectful.

This book is for us as well as for you. We are not perfect. We fall into some of the Traps in this book, too. We *know* the healthier way to act but still *act* in unhealthy ways at times. But it has always been reassuring for us to *know* that there is another way. To have *choices.* To admit who we are, weak or strong. To accept guidance. To learn from others. To value respect. We respect ourselves first. Then we respect each other. And the ups and downs become gifts, for which we are grateful.

Recovery is truly a gift. It means having humility instead of being a victim. It means being grateful rather than grandiose. Recovery means being powerful and respectful, not cruel.

For many of us, moving toward health *feels* cruel at first be-cause we never learned the difference between *enabling* and *respectful love* as we grew up in our families.

For example, we do everything for our kids because no one did anything for us when we were little, and then we realize our kids are spoiled and helpless. Even worse, we realize our kids are emotionally disabled — they can't feel a feeling, take out the garbage or pay their rent after they leave home. It will be hard to admit that we have made some parenting mistakes. But if we truly love ourselves and our kids, we will *act* on our new insight whether it comes when we are 30 years old or when we are 80 years old. We don't need to beat ourselves up for waiting until we were 80 to see the light.

We need to have the courage and respect to stop abusing and enabling when we finally see that we are abusing and enabling.

Because recovery feels cruel at first, many of us choose to stop our recovery for a while. We take one step backwards and breathe a sigh of relief. Some of us choose to stay back for good, finding "creative" ways to re-enact indefinitely the original system from which we came. For the rest of us who choose to risk something new, there *are* rewards down the road.

And there is another side to the Iceberg in our model. If we *risk* enough to find people we can *trust* on a regular basis, and if we *risk* enough to be *separate* and alone when we need to be, and if we *risk* enough to *respect* ourselves and others instead of enabling, then the gifts will start to flow.

In Figure 3.2, we show the other side — *The Iceberg Of Functional Health.* If we get into recovery, do the painful but rewarding family-of-origin work that we all must do, and make the initially painful decisions we must make to stop being co-dependent in our *present* lives, then the *Iceberg Of Co-dependency And Addictions* over the years gradually becomes the *Iceberg Of Functional Health.* Our diseases of addiction, compulsion, stress disorders, etc., begin to fade and are replaced with Self-Care, Respect, a solid and Safe Support System, proper Diet, Exercise and Sleep. Our underlying co-dependency issues of stuck identity and pseudo-intimacy are replaced with a Clear Identity and Healthy Intimacy. And changes happen deep inside of our personalities as well — beneath the Iceberg. Unhealthy Guilt is replaced by Respect, good Decision-Making, the ability to take the Initia-

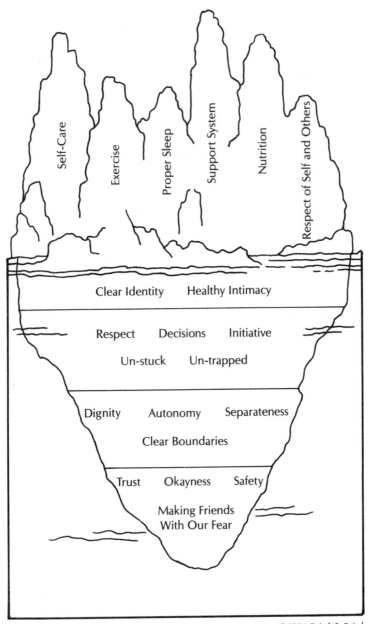

©1984 Friel & Friel

**Figure 3.2. The Iceberg Of Functional Health —
What Happens To Us When We Get Into Recovery**

tive and get Unstuck, and the ability to see and feel Traps and to avoid them or get out of them quickly. Unhealthy shame gradually diminishes, and we develop a strong sense of Dignity and Worth, Autonomy and Separateness, and Clear, Flexible Boundaries. And lastly, the deep sense of Mistrust and Fear of Abandonment slowly becomes a deep sense of Trust, Okayness and Safety, *despite the fact that we do not always get what we want from life.*

As so many of us have already experienced, we begin our journey of recovery with a lot of shame, hurt, pain, sadness and anger. We blame everyone else for our unhappiness. We lash out either as offenders or as manipulative victims always ready to blame others for our misery. As we get deeper and deeper into recovery, we find these feelings and beliefs and attitudes transforming into health. Recovery means moving *from shame and blame to respect and healthy love.* Recovery may be painful. Avoiding or getting out of Co-dependency/Adult Child Traps may hurt *at first.* But *we'll* take respect and healthy love over shame and blame any day. We *can* learn to be **functional**!

4

Caught In A Trap
Or Living A Life?

Changing our patterns of feelings and actions is hard. After all, we grew up this way, day after day after day. "Normal" is whatever we're used to and "healthy" is just a fantasy in self-help books. We laugh when we ask, "Is there such a thing as a healthy family?" And yet at some deep unconscious level we know that there *is* such a thing as a healthy family, and that just frustrates us all the more.

We grope around in the dark, floundering in our dysfunction, overwhelmed by our guilt and shame and fear. We watch other people whom we *think* might be healthy. We imitate what we *think* they might do to solve the problem that's bothering us, then we get even more frustrated and hopeless when it doesn't work out. Or worse, we may even *know* in our heads what the healthy thing is, but can't seem to bring ourselves to do it.

We read parenting books and recovery books and "how-to" books and have all the answers for our friends and colleagues. But when it comes to us, we can't seem to pull it off. This is because "knowing in our heads" is not enough. We must also have conviction in our hearts and our guts. Words are cheap. Actions are what count.

The biggest Trap of all is to be in total denial. As the veil of denial begins to lift and we get into recovery, the Traps gradually become more and more visible to us. We stumble through the early stages of recovery like toddlers learning to walk. We fall down. We pick ourselves up again. We get frustrated and want to quit. We try again. Then some more Traps become visible. We find ourselves stepping into fewer and fewer Traps. Then one day we awaken and find ourselves saying, "I *like* my life." We blink and pinch ourselves to see if we're dreaming. We check in with our feelings. "Yes," we say, "I *like* my life. I like myself!"

Stages Of Recovery

1. The Stage Of Oblivion

This is the typically long period in our lives when we are in complete denial that we came from a dysfunctional family or that we have any addictions, compulsions or symptoms. We may be like Pollyanna about our lives and our relationships. We smile and say that everything is "fine." We wear the mask of co-dependency — looking good on the surface but hurting inside. We may look unhealthy to others but be good at keeping others from giving us feedback. Whatever our trick is for staying in denial, we are in denial nonetheless. Usually our lives start to show signs of strain and wear and tear somewhere between the ages of 25 and 45, then we go into the next stage.

2. Crisis Management

Something finally snaps enough for us to identify that some kind of problem exists. Still pretty much in denial, though, we try to isolate the problem in our heads. We try to contain it and define it as more limited than it truly is.

"My wife is unhappy. Oh, well, she just needs to get out of the house more often."

"My son is using cocaine. Oh, well, he's just at that age when kids experiment a lot."

"I've been stressed out a lot lately. Oh, well, it will pass as soon as I get this project done."

"I find myself getting very interested in other men lately. Oh, well, I won't say anything to my husband. It will probably go away."

Each one of these statements, taken by itself, is not necessarily a big problem. But if we are in denial about a much deeper family system issue, the problem won't go away. In that case, we may seek outside help.

We may go from one therapist to another, seeking one who sees the problem as limited, the way we see it. We try to fix the problem with logic. We become excellent problem-solvers. We make charts of behavior. We make lists. We stay up late into the night with our spouse, lover or friends, analyzing and talking *about* problems. But the problem doesn't go away. We are in crisis, and we are doing crisis management, but the crisis doesn't go away. It has become *unmanageable*.

3. The Recovery Decision

It may take months or it may take years to reach this stage. This is the point at which we say, "My life has become unmanageable." I need to admit that there is a deep-seated problem here that isn't going to be fixed by some simple behavior modification. I need help. I need to do some deeper therapy work. I need to get into a 12-Step group.

Two things happen during this stage. First, we feel like failures and we feel a lot of fear and shame. Second, as we share these feelings with others, the fear and shame and sense of failure begin to lift. We feel an initial burst of relief. We start to get better and healthier. Within a few months we realize that there is something inside of us, our Little Child, that needs to be allowed to heal. This brings us to the next stage in our recovery.

4. Family-Of-Origin/Feelings Work

We have seen few people, ourselves included, who could do this stage without professional help. And while 12-Step groups are a mandatory part of the work that we do with our clients, even these groups do not seem to be enough to do the deeper healing that needs to be done. At some point most of us have to do some family-of-origin and feelings work in a *group therapy* setting for this deep healing to take place. Why? Because this work must be done in a very safe place; and some of it can be scary. In our Lifeworks Clinic which we offer around the country, we see this process of healing as going through the following steps (Kellogg).

1. We need to **identify** the wrongs that happened to us as children.
2. We need to **have our feelings** about those wrongs, not just talk about them.
3. We need to **embrace** those feelings, i.e., let them become as big as they really were back then.
4. We need to **share** those feelings with others, not just talk about them with others.
5. We need to **make a decision** about our relationship with the person or people who hurt us and who continue to hurt us.
6. **Then** we can begin to heal and forgive. **Not before.**

As you begin looking for a therapist or treatment program to do this kind of work, ask around. Be an informed consumer. If this is the kind of work that you want or need to do, ask the therapist or treatment center *directly* to see if they know how to do this kind of work.

5. Healing The Self

For most of us, family-of-origin/feelings work is done on and off for one to four years. We may attend a short-term intensive treatment process and do a big chunk of work around family of origin, and then spend some time integrating what we've learned into our daily lives. Then another big chunk will come up and we may work on that in our ongoing therapy group. At some point in this process, we may start to notice that we feel better, in little but significant ways, right down to our toes. We listen to our Little Child more often. And we start to heal.

6. *Integration Into Daily Living*

Only when we have started to heal from the inside out are we ready to apply the suggestions and examples contained in this book. Until then, we may *know* that we have the right to get off the phone when someone is boring us or trying to make us into their therapist, but we won't be able to do it. Our Guilt, Shame and Fear of Abandonment will always be tripping us up.

5

Basic Principles Of
Functional Living

We will present short chapters on problems in daily living that face all of us *all* the time, along with pointers on how to deal with them. In some cases the suggestions will be in the form of simple stories. In others they will be lists. Or we may just present problems and offer some ways that we and others have handled them satisfactorily in the past. It is up to you to decide whether our suggestions will work for you or not. But before we go further, we need to tell you what this book is *really* about. At one level it is simply a cookbook, but at another level it is about the following Principles Of Functional Living.

Principles Of Functional Living

1. *Boundaries*

Boundaries represent the core of this book. For a lengthier discussion of boundaries, see *Adult Children: The Secrets Of Dysfunctional Families* (Friel & Friel, 1988). But briefly, boundaries are like the fence around our yard or the walls and doors enclosing our house. Examples of boundaries include:

29

1. Physical   5. Social
2. Intellectual   6. Time
3. Emotional   7. Money
4. Sexual

Our **physical boundaries** are violated whenever someone touches us, hits us, goes into our house or our room, reads our diary, snoops through our personal effects, uses our tools or our hair dryer, tickles us, etc., etc., etc., *when we don't want them to.* Sometimes a physical boundary violation also can be a sexual, emotional, money, time or intellectual boundary violation. In fact, all of these boundaries overlap one another quite a bit.

An **intellectual boundary** violation happens when someone "gets into our heads" and tries to *discount* or *steal* what we think. "Oh, why do you think *that?*" "You don't think that pollution is a problem, do you?" "How could you think *that?*"

Our **emotional boundaries** get violated when our feelings are *discounted, ignored, criticized, belittled* and *taken for granted.* "How could you feel that!?" "You don't feel sad, do you?" "Wipe that smile off your face." "I'll give you something to cry about." "I can't be around you when you cry." "You have no *right* to be angry."

Our **social boundaries** include those we choose to be with and under what circumstances. "You don't like large parties? What's the matter with you?" "You don't like Joe or Kim? What's the matter with you?"

Sexual boundaries have a lot to do with privacy, what we choose to do with or have done to our bodies, those we choose to do it with, how we are touched and by whom. It is obvious that rape is a sexual boundary violation. It is not so obvious that having someone stare and leer at us in an objectifying way is also a sexual boundary violation.

Time boundaries have to do with our comfort level for getting things done in the world. Some of us thrive on deadlines and "being almost late," while others of us need to have a buffer of time between things that we do. Some of us need two hours to get

ready in the morning, and others of us need 30 minutes. All of us
need to respect our own and others' boundaries around time.

Money boundaries have to do with how we spend it, how we
save it, what we do with it, and how much of it we need to earn
to feel safe.

Boundaries are set by saying "yes" or "no." When we say "yes"
but really feel like saying "no," we have stepped into a Trap. When
we say "no" when we really wanted to say "yes," we have stepped
into a Trap. Having clear, flexible boundaries is the key to having
a clear, flexible identity.

2. Feelings

Our *true* feelings, rather than what we convince ourselves we
should be feeling, provide the keys to unlocking the door to
recovery. We like the saying, *"don't should on yourself."*

3. Respect

Respect is *not* impulsive and it is *not* enabling or caretaking.
Respect is powerful, honest, true, warm, lonely at times, firm,
forgiving and thoughtful. Respect assumes that we are both human and we are both responsible for our own lives. Respect
assumes that we each have the power to make our own choices.
Respect assumes that we each have to live our own choices.
Respect assumes that we can make mistakes and change our
choices. Respect is spontaneous. It is not *too responsible* and it is
not *irresponsible*. We respect ourselves first, and from that flows
respect of others.

4. Love

Love is a respectful response from one human being to another.
It is care without enmeshment. It is responsible without being
compulsive and worrying. It is filled with hope. It is honest. Love
is "owning" our joy and pain while observing and recognizing
others' joy and pain. Love doesn't hurt, but sometimes the choices
we must make as loving people do hurt.

5. Rights

We have the right to life, liberty and the pursuit of happiness
in this country. We have the right to pursue love. We have the
right to feel what we feel without being criticized or ignored, we
have the right to think what we think without being put on a
debate team, we have the right to set our own boundaries, we
have the right to go where we want to go and do what we want
to do. And inextricably connected with rights we also have
responsibilities . . .

6. Responsibilities

With every right comes a responsibility. We have the right to
conceive and bear children, but then we have a responsibility to
raise them. We have the right to say no, but then we have the
responsibility to ourselves and the other person to follow through
with the consequences of saying no. We have the right to get
married, but then we have the responsibility to "be in that marriage" or, if we can't anymore, to get out of it. We have the right
to have sexual intercourse with each other, but we have the
responsibility to be honest, caring and respectful with each other
when we do it. We have the right to defend ourselves, but we
have the responsibility to do it in a respectful way.

7. Beliefs

As children we took on many beliefs from our families. Some
of us took on the belief that all people are good, or that all people
are bad. Some of us took on the belief that a good person always
gives, even if it means hurting other people. Some of us believe
that we have to be loved by *everyone* before we can be okay. Some
of us believe that religion is bad, or that *our* religion is the only
one that is good.

We believe that beliefs can get in the way of our recovery
sometimes. Is that confusing? We believe so. As recovering people,
as authors and as therapists, *we know* that belief systems can
block recovery. If I believe that I can *only* be a good person if I

help others (to the exclusion of helping myself), then I am in big trouble. If I believe that God is an angry, critical man with a beard who sits on the clouds and punishes, then I am in trouble. If I believe that a good person must make a lot of money, or must stuff his or her anger, or must focus on his or her children to the exclusion of self, then I am in trouble.

As adults our major "growing-up task" is to figure out which beliefs we want to believe. Internationally known and respected psychotherapist Albert Ellis has developed an entire system of therapy based on our irrational belief systems.

8. Actions

As we work through our Co-dependency/Adult Child Traps, it is absolutely *critical* that we start focusing on *actions* rather than words. Mind Games, Mind Rape, Manipulation, Tricks, Traps, Hooks, You-Name-It. There *is* a bottom line, and it is action. *What we do.* I say, "I love only you," but I am having a sexual or emotional affair on the side. I say, "I am an involved, caring father," but I never spend any time with my kids. I say, "We are good friends," but I never call you for lunch. I say, "I am flexible and open to change," but I sabotage and undermine every attempt at change that comes from me or you by saying, "I'd like to, but . . . " or "We could do that but . . . " or "Sure, we can do that, as long as *you* realize that if we do it . . ." Look at what folks do, not what they say.

9. Decisions

As recovering or unrecovering people, we make tons of decisions every day. "I'm not going to let Mom get to me *anymore!*" "Dad hurts me when he does that." "This is going to stop!" "I love Jane, but I can't take her affair *anymore!*" *Decisions* are easy to make. Following through with decisions is something else again. If you find yourself making hundreds of decisions but following through with few of them, go back to step one. "My life has become unmanageable. I am powerless over this mess." Actions speak louder than words. Decisions happen in our heads. We vote with our feet.

10. Power

This one is *very* confusing for most of us. We see it and want it, we've been hurt by it time and again, and we embrace it and recoil from it at the same time. If we're female, we say, "I want power! I'm tired of being used." If we're traditional males, we say, "To hell with power. I'm going to *yield* from now on." Women begin to get angry and demanding. Men start being passive and wimpy. And lover/spouse relationships continue to be confusing. Good grief! When does it all stop? If history has any wisdom, the answer is "never." Whether gay or straight, rich or poor, wise or foolish, one thing is true — balancing power is a problem.

Struggles for power mean nothing unless they are framed in the context of personal recovery. There are so many levels of power that we could write books for two million years before we even began to get a handle on them. Our *struggles with power* must be put in the context of our own childhoods. Are we battling with an ex-spouse about our child's health and well-being, or are we *really* battling about how I got used as a kid? Do I *really* care about being late all the time, or is it more about how no one ever took *me* seriously when I was growing up? Is my *overkill-caring-about-my-kids* about my belief that we should over-kill our kids with care, or is it about the painful truth that as a kid, I didn't get my needs met?

Healthy power feels whole. It feels respectful of self and others. When we are truly powerful, we don't have to *use* other people. We can say "no" and still care. We can say "yes" and feel safe. We can accept our alone-ness when it happens, and still go on with life. We can get what we need from life. We can continue with our recovery and still feel connected to other human beings. Above all, *we can stop being wimpy and rageful.*

11. Paradoxes

A paradox is something that *seems* to be a contradiction, but in *fact* is *not*. In truth, we can love and hate someone at the same time. We can be powerful by yielding. We can be weak by continuing the fight. We can be surrounded by people and be lonely. We can be alone and feel full. At some point in our recovery we start to *transcend* these paradoxes. We don't rise above them. We begin to *make sense* out of them.

Feeling healthy and whole means that we are *comfortable* with paradoxes. "I don't know what it all means. I love her a lot, and I get really angry at her sometimes, too. I even hate her sometimes. That's life!" Or we might say, "I am not good all the time. Sometimes I am bad. Naughty, even. But I am a good person." Catch yourself trying to put the world into boxes and pigeonholes. When you can laugh and say, "Oh, it doesn't *fit* into pigeonholes," then you are on your way to recovery!

6

The Wisdom Of
The Bear

Once upon a time there was a big Brown Bear who lived peacefully in the woods near a clear rushing stream. He liked where he lived. He liked the fresh clean air, the abundance of fish in the nearby stream, the dappled sunlight beneath the tall pine trees, the open meadows and the cool damp forest. Every day was filled with quiet time snoozing in the sun on his favorite granite rock by the stream; the challenges of searching for food and romping with his mate.

One day as he was ambling down to the stream for a drink of clear icy water, something happened. WHACK! A searing pain pulsed through his foot. He lunged forward to escape. THUD! He was trapped to the earth by a pair of steel jaws and a thick metal chain pounded deep into the earth.

"No!" shouted the big Brown Bear. "It's a bear trap."

His paws weren't really built to spread the jaws of a bear trap, and his brain wasn't really built to figure this out at all. He was in a bad situation.

After several hours of painful struggle, the big Brown Bear had mangled his foot almost to shreds. There was blood everywhere.

He called for his mate, who finally heard his calls, but there was nothing she could do either. So she sat patiently next to him to give him comfort, crying quietly and hoping for a miracle.

Finally, after several more hours, his mangled foot jerked free from the trap, and he crawled sadly away from that place and back into the woods. His mate stayed behind for awhile to try to understand how this had happened, but nothing came to her. Her brain wasn't really designed to figure these things out either.

At last, she returned to their den, where the big Brown Bear was nursing his mangled foot as best he could. They stayed up most of the night, discussing what had happened to them that day, but neither of them could make head nor tail of it. And so with what brain capacity they did have, they simply decided never to return to that place in the woods again. And so they didn't.

PART II

Getting Unhooked

The dogmas of the quiet past are inadequate to the stormy present . . . As our case is new, so we must think anew and act anew.

Abraham Lincoln
Message to Congress
December 1, 1862

7

Where's The Manual For This Family? (Overt And Covert Rules)

Picture this. You're a newborn infant. You just entered the world, got cleaned up and started nursing, and you're feeling warm and safe and comfortable. A few days into this nice routine, your excited parents wrap you up, take you into the family car and drive you to your new home. This is great! This is my family! Your parents want you to fit in right away and so do you. But you're just a baby, remember. You can barely focus your little eyes. You can't hold your head up, and when you try, your head wobbles around and your eyes spin inside their little sockets. Oh, well, growing up takes time.

And then the big surprise hits! Your parents prop you up in one of those infant seats that's sitting on the kitchen table. They look at you with those silly, proud grins that new parents make, and you look back warmly, although somewhat unfocused. And then, right before your eyes, they place on the table a thick, 500-page manual in which are contained the thousands of rules and regulations that you will need to know if you want to "fit in just right" in this family of yours. You don't know it yet, but inside are things like: "It's okay to get angry and laugh, but we won't feel comfortable if you cry when you're sad. In fact, if you get too moody or sad when you're growing up, we will bring you lots of food or drugs or things to distract you from your feelings, so that *we* will feel more comfortable. We will tell you, or at least let you conclude, that we are doing it to make you feel better, but that won't be true. We're really teaching you to be addicted so that we won't have to deal with *our* discomfort with your natural, human feelings. And then, when you grow up, if you ever do, and you try to figure this all out by getting into therapy, we will confuse you even more by saying we're glad you're in therapy because we've known all along that you've been 'different' and that *you've* had a problem. This will make it next to impossible for you to ever figure out that it was *us* in the first place who set you up to overeat or drink or buy things compulsively and to be uncomfortable with your feelings."

Wow! What a long, complicated rule! Wow! What a tortuous, complicated, deeply hidden plot line. Wow! What the heck *is* this thing in front of me? A manual? What's a manual? Read? I can barely see! And then your parents say to you, "We want you to learn how to fit into this family just right, so we want you to read and memorize all of the rules in this 500-page manual by Friday, and then we'll give you a multiple-choice and essay exam on the rules. We'll give you three chances to pass the exam."

In some ways, such a manual would make recovery much easier, because what it would do is to make the *covert* rules in our family systems come out into the open and become *overt*. And you know, what we just did above *will* make a covert rule overt for some of you. And that *is* what recovery is about. Making the covert, overt. Making what's hidden come out into the open. What we say in our Lifeworks Clinic Process is that **nothing changes until it becomes real.**

Unfortunately, we don't have such manuals. We *do* learn all of those rules, but the way that we learn them is really done by "osmosis," as many of us put it. It is a hypnotic process of rule-learning, in which, day after day, month after month, year after year, we are exposed to the behavior, facial expressions, eye movements, body language, smiles, frowns, grunts, cries, tears, rages and other feelings and behaviors of our family members. And it doesn't take long to learn the rules.

We go to our first funeral with Dad and Mom when we are six, for example, and we look up into the faces of all those big adults around us. We feel sad, scared, lonely, etc., but as we look up into those faces, we don't see any tears. We *feel* like crying, but we keep looking into those adult faces and we see no tears. So we follow the rules — we don't cry. See how it works? Nobody *ever* has to say, "We don't allow crying in this family." We just figure it out, because human children are very smart and our brains are pre-wired to pick up on these cues.

So we have learned *covertly* that it's not okay to cry. And we therefore can *never heal from losses.* But when someone asks us or our parents if we had a healthy family and if we were able to express our feelings, Dad or Mom will say, "Why, of course we did. We *always* believed in healthy expression of feeling." (Dad and Mom may have *talked about* feelings, which is nothing like *having* their feelings.) And so the *overt* rule was very different than the *covert* one.

Where's the manual for this family? It's all around us, every day, in those overt and covert behaviors of Dad and Mom and everyone else. But it's hard to go back and figure out what those rules were, because they were all absorbed into our *unconscious* as we went about our everyday tasks of growing up. So when you wonder why you do some of the painful things that you do, like reach for that piece of pie when you get "dangerously close to a feeling" (Pietrini, 1988), remember that you learned to do that somewhere. You will continue to *re-enact* or repeat that pattern until you first figure out where you learned it and then have your feelings about it and about the folks who taught it to you.

If you find yourself unable to set some of the boundaries suggested by this book, take some time to go back and look at the manual for your family. Some examples of how this works are as follows:

How Did I Learn To Be So Self-Destructive?

1. By watching Mom take care of everyone else but herself.
2. By watching Dad smoke or drink or work himself to death.

3. By being hit or battered or shamed or criticized.
4. By seeing my brother or sister be ridiculed unmercifully by Dad or Mom.
5. By experiencing little care or concern from others when I was a little child.
6. By being told to "always keep a stiff upper lip" when I was hurting emotionally or physically.
7. By being given food whenever my feelings appeared.

How Did I Learn To Let People Use Me And Violate Me?

1. Because Dad or Mom didn't respect my privacy or boundaries; they read my personal diary or journal, they snooped through my closets or drawers, they physically abused me, they shared their personal problems with me instead of dealing with them themselves, they made me their "pal," etc.
2. By watching Dad let Mom emotionally abuse him.
3. By watching Mom let Dad physically abuse her.
4. By watching Dad or Mom stay on the phone for hours with someone they didn't want to talk to because Dad or Mom was so "nice."
5. By watching Dad let people take advantage of him in business.
6. By watching Mom be "nice" to uninvited houseguests for days and days when inside she was deeply resentful and angry.
7. By watching Dad or Mom go from one seductive, abusive love relationship to another.

When you're getting stuck, go back to the manual. Find the rules. Admit that you're repeating the pattern all over again. Have your feelings about being a victim. Share those feelings with others whom you can trust. Then make the difficult changes. And *expect to feel guilty when you try to set boundaries.*

8

Unhooking
Pointers

To get Unhooked from Co-dependency/Adult Child Traps, to avoid those Traps or get out of them, we all need to learn the following process.

1. **Stop!** Don't make a decision, don't say yes or no, until you've gone through each of these steps.
2. Connect with your inner self, your Little Child — and do it *uncritically*.
3. Feel your feelings. Let your feelings become "red flags" or warning signals.
4. Check in with your support system. Share those feelings no matter how silly you *think* they are.
5. *Then think* and *plan ahead*. Not planning ahead is one of the best ways to keep stepping into Traps.

To exemplify this process, let's take a look at how Sharon handled it. Sharon has been in recovery for four years. She went to inpatient treatment for her Co-dependency/Adult Child issues and has been in a therapy group for the past 18 months. Sharon's friend Liz has done some therapy work in bits and pieces but she hasn't got down to her deeper issues yet. Liz is in the middle of a very painful, destructive relationship with her lover. She has called Sharon three times this week, usually after 10:00 p.m., to tell her how bad the relationship has become and how much it hurts. Sharon is beginning to feel overwhelmed, confused, scared and angry, but she doesn't want to hurt Liz's feelings. Her old self is starting to do battle with her new self. The two Icebergs are bumping up against each other.

Sharon hung up the phone at 12:30 a.m. after the third call and said to herself, **"Stop!"** She took a deep breath, relaxed in the chair she was sitting in, and began listening to her feelings. She did not try to think about what must be done. She just sat in a darkened room and listened to her feelings.

The next day she checked in with some friends and got some feedback about her feelings. Her friends were supportive of her feelings, but did not try to offer her any solutions. In fact, Sharon said at the beginning, "I just need to have you hear how I'm feeling. I don't need any solutions." Her friends respected her request.

Her feelings sent up red flags all over the place. She wasn't getting enough rest, she was becoming preoccupied with Liz's problem, she was getting angry and confused. It felt like the Old Iceberg was moving in for the kill. The Titanic was about to sink a second time.

Then Sharon thought it through. "I must *take care of myself* first. But I must be *respectful* too. I may *lose* my friendship with Liz. What will I do to fill that gap if Liz chooses to end the friendship because I am honest with her? I will feel sad. Rejected. Abandoned. Scared. Ashamed. Guilty. Can I face those feelings again? I need to be sure to get myself around some other people in recovery on the day that I talk to Liz about this."

And then Sharon made a decision to talk to Liz about it. It didn't happen on Sharon's schedule, though. Liz called her at 6:00 p.m. the next day, in tears and suicidal. Sobbing, Liz began by saying, "Sharon, I have to come over and see you. It's just awful! I don't think I can take it any longer. I . . ." Sharon firmly but gently interrupted, "Liz, I have something to say to you." Then Liz interrupted, "Sharon, I have to see you!" And Sharon came back firmly, "Liz, I care a lot about you. What's happening to you scares me but I'm not equipped to handle this anymore. I'm not a therapist." Liz screamed, "Oh, don't give me that crap. You think I'm crazy, huh? Well, I'll show you!" Sharon said, "If you're suicidal, I'll take you down to the emergency room of the hospital, and I'll be there for you if you need me. If you're not suicidal, I can give you the name of a therapist, or get you the names of some others I know are good. But I can't be your therapist."

Liz slammed down the receiver on the phone and Sharon heard a deadly "click" and then a dial tone. Sharon's guts wrenched. Waves of guilt swept over her. Fear engulfed her. And then she listened to her Little Child again. Her Little Child inside of her said, "You have taken good care of us these past two years. I feel better when you listen to me. It has been good to see us both get so healthy. We have lived a whole life of pain and enmeshment in other people's problems. You have been respectful with Liz. Liz is an adult. She is the only one who can control her life. You have been an honorable, respectful person. You are a good person." Sharon listened. She finished cooking dinner, ate, cleaned up her apartment, watched the news on TV and went to sleep.

The next morning, Sharon was awakened by the telephone ringing. The voice at the other end was reassuring and calm.

"Sharon?"

"Yes, this is Sharon," she replied, waking up a bit as she spoke.

"This is Karen Johnson. I'm the intake coordinator at Lincoln Hospital. Your friend Liz has given me permission to contact you and tell you that she is all right. She took an overdose of Valium last night, but called 911 just before she passed out. She's stable now and has made a commitment to work on this problem with us." Tears of relief, joy and health welled up in Sharon's eyes. "Thank you for calling, Karen," Sharon replied. "You're welcome, Sharon."

Getting unhooked is not easy, especially at first. The road to health can feel cruel in the beginning. We will stumble and fall sometimes as we try to get healthy; but if we keep trying, we will eventually succeed. There *are* no failures in life. Life is something we participate in and learn from, if we are open to it. Every day we are faced with chances to choose health or choose Traps. And every day provides us the chance to get out of an Old Trap or to avoid a new one. The work is painful, but the rewards are great.

In Figure 8.1 we reproduce here the Recovery Process Flow Chart that was published at the end of our first book. *Use this flow chart whenever you feel stuck, lost, confused, "crazy," as if you're in the beginning of a slip or relapse back into old patterns or addictions; and when you feel hopeless or helpless.* So many of us start to do extremely well in our growing up and then we gradually start to slip back into our old patterns until one day we wake up and feel as if we've gone right back to the beginning of our pain. Using this flow chart will let your brain tell you when your emotions or your life are getting out of control.

Figure 8.1. Recovery Process Flow Chart

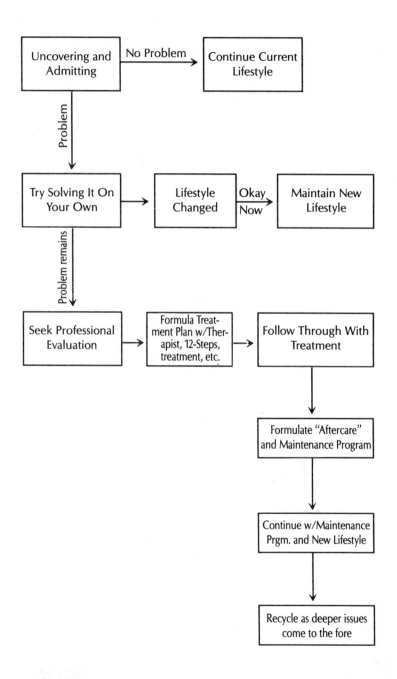

PART III

Taking Care
Of The One
Who's In Charge

Children have neither a past nor a future. Thus they
enjoy the present — which seldom happens to us.

Jean de la Bruyere
Caracteres, XI, 1688

9

Feelings
(What *Am* I Feeling?)

Problem

Sometimes we just don't know what we're feeling. If we grew up in a dysfunctional home, we probably don't know how we feel much of the time. Someone asks us to do something and we don't know how we feel about it. We experience a loss and go numb. We experience a success and remain stone-faced. The reality is, of course, that we are always feeling something. Feelings are the body's normal reactions to events outside of us as well as to events that occur inside of our minds. And feelings occur *in the body*. The problem is that we have learned to *not notice* our feelings. We have learned to *not pay attention to them*. The problem is that we do certain things that *block* our noticing of our feelings.

Feeling Blockers

We won't be able to notice our feelings very well if we . . .

- are drinking alcohol
- are eating compulsively
- work too much
- jog all the time
- go up into our heads to try to "figure it out"
- get defensive and distort our feelings, or turn them into another feeling (like when we get mad when we're really hurt or sad or scared)
- etc.; etc., etc.

Feelings And What They Feel Like

Anger

A feeling of power in the gut is followed by a surge of muscle tension in the lower, middle and upper back and shoulders followed by a rush of adrenalin and blood flow throughout the body.

Sadness

A little empty feeling begins to localize in the throat and head and finally builds until we begin to cry. Also a hollow feeling in the upper chest and gut is experienced especially when deep loss has been experienced or re-experienced.

Joy

An overall sense of exhilaration, a feeling of lightness and healthy power and spirituality is felt. A surge of adrenalin seems to enhance our sense of self and our connectedness with the universe. We feel warm all over.

Hurt

A pit in the stomach, as if we've been kicked in the gut is felt plus a feeling of violation, betrayal or pain.

Shame

At its deepest level, shame is experienced in the lower gut and genital area. It is a feeling of being broken, defective, unworthy, unlovable, stupid, ugly, dirty, awful, bad, evil, crazy or worthless. The bigger the shame, the more likely it is that we are carrying the shame *for* someone else or *for* the entire family system from which we came.

Fear

Fear is felt in the upper chest and breathing passages. It is a sense that somehow our life and survival are being threatened. It is felt as a sense of dread and anxiety which eventually spreads throughout the entire body.

Loneliness

A feeling of being separate, disconnected, empty, devoid of human contact and companionship is experienced.

Guilt

A heavy burden or responsibility urges us to *act* to correct some real or imagined wrong.

Safety

A warm, comfortable feeling of "okay-ness," connectedness.

As you go about your day, begin to pay attention to your feelings. Check in with yourself before you act impulsively. Let your feelings *speak to you.* They will tell you wondrous things! Stop, breathe deeply and just let the feelings percolate up to the surface of your conscious awareness. *Notice* your breathing. *Notice* the quickening pulse of your fear or your joy. *Notice* how tight your muscles became or how flushed you just became. Our feelings are all there for a purpose. They can help to guide us if we listen to them.

It is important to remember, too, that in our dysfunction we can't always trust our first impressions of feelings. We may trust abusers at first. We may feel safe when it's really dangerous. But as we notice our bodies and their messages more and more each day, we also will begin to be able to trust our feelings. Give it a try. It's worth a notice.

10

Accept The Unexpected

Problem:

My car breaks down on the way to an appointment. Our vacation falls through when one of us gets sick. My souffle collapses just before the guests arrive. My child picks the one college major I wished he wouldn't. My flight is cancelled.

What I Am Feeling Inside:

Frustrated, angry, scared, disappointed, defeated, let down, anxious, nervous, embarrassed, guilty, worried, victimized by life, hopeless.

My Old Beliefs:

Life is always fair if I try hard enough and do it right. I can control most everything if I am vigilant enough. It's my fault . . . If only I had . . . It's their fault.

What I Used To Do Or Still Do Now:

Rage, scream, give up, escalate my blood pressure, blame others, lash out, initiate hundreds of lawsuits, tear myself down.

Where Or Why We May Still Be Stuck:

Life is *not* always fair. Life is *not* always predictable. We cannot control events around us that are beyond our control. This is one of the earliest truths we learn in our families; and if the family is healthy, we learn to live with that truth well. If our family is dysfunctional, we learn to do battle with this truth — either by beating ourselves up by lashing out at others or by trying to control others in ways they don't want to be controlled.

In unhealthy families, we see Dad and Mom being rigid and fearful of change. We watch them rage or pace the floor in knots of anxiety when life plays tricks on them. We see them obsess, drink, eat, smoke or go without sleep when things don't go according to plan.

In healthy families, we learn two important things which are related to this problem:

1. We learn to change the things we can.
2. We learn to accept the things we cannot change — the essence of the Serenity Prayer.

Surrender is as important to emotional health as is *going after what we want.* But these two must be in balance.

In dysfunctional families, we either give up too easily or we fight losing battles or both. If we are still doing this today, we need to ask ourselves, "Where did I learn this? From Dad? Mom? Both? How am I still *unconsciously* bonded to Dad or Mom? Or to my entire family system?" We need to realize that we are *powerless* over the rules of that bigger system from which we came. We will *then* be able to handle the unexpected gracefully and peacefully.

Battling with the unexpected things in life is almost always about our deep-seated *fear* of abandonment (by self or others). There is always shame involved. And we often blame ourselves or others because we don't want to admit our powerlessness.

If a tornado hits my house, I *could* start thinking, "If only I'd been home earlier, I could have saved more of the house!" Really! How? By standing in front of the tornado and shaking my fist at it? Sounds silly, doesn't it? But that's just how we think when life plays tricks on us and we don't yet know how to roll with the punches.

Some New Beliefs To Try:

In any given week, some things will inevitably go wrong.
The world isn't perfect.
I am not God.
Sometimes there's no one to blame.

New Things To Do Or Try:

Say the Serenity Prayer.
Order out for pizza or eat the fallen souffle as is.
Laugh about it.
Catch up on your journaling or call some old friends if you're stuck in the airport.
Let go of the vacation for now and say, "It was meant to be."
Meditate.
Be thankful your son is excited about his college major.

Affirmation

I am in healthy recovery. I know that things will go wrong. I am okay even when things around me aren't working out as I had planned. The unexpected things in life give me opportunities to use my new-found emotional health.

11

When I'm
Lonely . . .

Loneliness goes right down to the depth of our souls. Learning to enjoy being alone (rather than lonely) is a sign of maturity and emotional health, up to a point. People who were Lost Children in their families when they were little sometimes enjoy being alone too much, so watch out for this one.

If you are aware that you are lonely, try some of the following . . .

1. Call a friend and talk for a while.
2. Write in your journal.
3. Sit quietly and embrace the loneliness for a while.
4. Write a poem to your loneliness.
5. Go to a movie, play or concert.
6. Tell yourself tomorrow will be a new day and that you will start taking the initiative more often to make sure you are with people part of each week or weekend.
7. Read a book.
8. Go to a 12-Step meeting.

9. If the loneliness gets deep, reach out and ask for help.
10. Realize that loneliness is always part of being human, and that if you try to have no loneliness in your life at all, you are fighting a losing battle.

Affirmation

Loneliness is part of being human. I can reach out and take risks to meet people, be with people and get closer to people. While I cannot make someone be close to me, I can increase my chances of getting close to others if I take the risk to do so.

12

All Stressed
Out With
Nowhere To Go

There has been so much written about stress that it seems stressful to write more about it. But it *is* important to understand how we react to stress, what stress is and some healthy and unhealthy things we can do about it.

Stress is the villain of the 20th century. Stress is out of control. Everyone is talking about stress! It is estimated that from 60 to 80 percent of all medical problems have a stress-related component to them. We all know, don't we, that stress can cause ulcers and high blood pressure? Stress is bad, right? Right. But stress is also good! Without some stress in our lives, we could not live. How can this be?

1. Stress is anything which causes the body's resources to be mobilized

With this definition, it is easy to see how the following can be stressful:

>   deadlines
>   losing your job
>   running into a grizzly bear in the woods

But with the same definition, these are also stressful:

    running one mile

    making love

    winning $1 million in a lottery

Stress experts speak of *positive stressors* and *negative stressors;* and to complicate matters, what is positive for one person may be negative for another. One busy executive may thrive on a 70-hour work schedule, while another may have a heart attack because of it. One person may need only five hours of sleep, while another needs nine hours to feel rested. Each of us has our own *optimal* stress needs. Too much stress can make us sick. Too little stress can leave us bored, apathetic and depressed. A life with absolutely *no demands* may be nice for a few days, but for an entire lifetime? Therefore:

2. Stressors Can Be Either Positive Or Negative.

3. We Need A Certain Level Of Stress Each Day.

4. The First Step In Controlling Stress Is To Honestly Take Your Own Inventory.

What Happens To Our Bodies Under Stress?

You are driving down an interstate highway on a rainy evening. Visibility is very poor and you are being more cautious than usual. You are a few minutes late for an important meeting and are a bit preoccupied with getting there on time. Suddenly the car in front of you skids out of control! It smashes into the guard-rail and flips over into your lane. You slam on your brakes and jerk the steering wheel to the left to avoid a crash. The front of your car catches the rear bumper of the disabled vehicle and you feel yourself thrown violently toward your windshield. Your seat belt and shoulder belt pull forcefully on your body, and then your car comes to a jolting halt. You and the other driver bolt from your automobiles and run to the shoulder of the road to avoid oncoming traffic.

Then you breathe a sigh of relief and you feel your legs trembling. You have survived!

This is a *clear-cut stressor*. It has a definite beginning and ending, and the body's reaction to it is very predictable. To handle a crisis like the one above, our bodies are programmed to do several things which give us added strength and alertness. Some of these bodily reactions are listed below.

Heart rate increases
Blood pressure increases
Blood sugar levels increase
Muscle tension increases
Brain activity increases
Digestion slows or stops
Peripheral blood vessels constrict

The idea here is that the body is now ready for an emergency. There is more blood available to the brain and muscles, and unimportant functions like digestion are slowed or stopped. The last reaction on this list, *constriction of peripheral blood vessels*, allows more blood to go to the muscles and brain and also reduces the risk of severe blood loss should the person be cut during the emergency. It also accounts for the fact that often we get *cold hands and feet when we are under stress*.

A Healthy Bodily Stress Reaction

Let's look at a person who has a healthy stress pattern as he or she goes through a typical day. As the day progresses, the following major stressors occur:

9:00 a.m. — Near accident on the freeway
11:00 a.m. — Disagreement with boss over policy
1:00 p.m. — Deadline for a report moved up three days
3:00 p.m. — Flight to New York delayed

With each stressor, the body reacts in predictable ways, as mentioned above, and then the body gets control of itself and returns to normal. In some cases, the body will go slightly below normal as it tries to regain its balance.

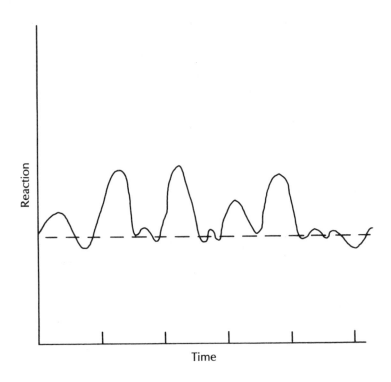

Figure 12.1. Healthy Bodily Stress Reaction

This is what happens when we are in control of our stress reactions and we somehow manage to keep the stressors *clear* in our own minds. When the stressors are too *vague,* and when our own bodily mechanisms have gotten out of control, then something else happens.

An Unhealthy Bodily Stress Reaction

When our bodies become *addicted to stress,* when our lifestyle has taught us that the only way to survive is to *stay mobilized* in the face of these *vague stressors,* we get *escalating stress.* The stress accumulates like an unhealthy negative bank balance until we can no longer maintain the physical roller-coaster that we are on. At this point, some sort of physical or emotional collapse occurs, as shown in Figure 12.2.

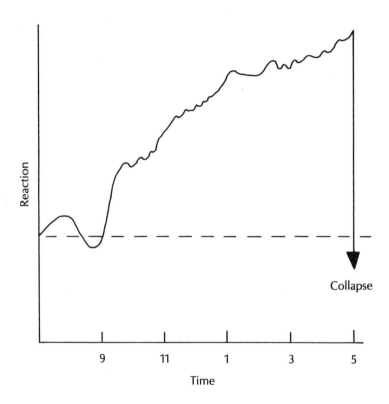

Figure 12.2. Unhealthy Bodily Stress Reaction

We hope this is not simply a dry, meaningless graph for you. Study it carefully, because when we allow this pattern to develop over a long period of time, the end result can be one or several of the following: Hypertension, tension headaches, colds and flu, migraine headaches, ulcers, colitis, depression, loss of interest in sex, heart disease, irritability, fatigue, alcoholism or alcohol abuse, other chemical dependency, apathy, lack of interest in people, family conflicts, temporomandibular joint disorder (TMD).

There are others, but the picture should be clear. One of the most insidious things about stress and burnout is that by the time we develop some of the more serious effects on this list, we have become so out of touch with ourselves we haven't the foggiest idea how we got there. It is our deepest hope that this book will prevent the above problems, and that if you have them, it will serve as a road map to help you move in the direction of better health.

Some Examples Of Stressors

This list of typical stressors has been helpful to some of our clients.

Career

Conflicts with superiors, subordinates or co-workers
Inefficient management of time
Problems in delegating authority
Too heavy a workload
Lacking the knowledge or training to do my job
Having too few challenges; being bored.

Partner

Not enough time together
Not enough time apart
Power struggles
Differences in values or expectations
Sexual concerns.

Kids

Discipline problems
Finding enough time to do things with them
Sibling rivalry
Interference from relatives
Seeing them as too much of a reflection on us.

Friends

Not enough
Too many acquaintances, not enough close friends
Demanding too much of my time
Take but don't give
Competitive or critical.

Other

Too many outside activities
Not enough "alone time"
All work and no play
All play and no work.

In looking at stressors in your life, remember that *you* must be the judge of what is too much and what is not enough. Just because your spouse says you need to do more of something or less of something, doesn't mean it's true for you. Remember also, that what is stressful for me may be energizing for you. There are **positive** and **negative stressors**, and only you can determine what those are for you.

Also remember that old dictum about too much of a good thing. Jogging can be very healthy, but all serious joggers know the signs of overdoing it, which include inability to sleep, irritability, fatigue, severe soreness and physical injury. Listening to your body and your inner self carefully will give you the answer. *Nothing else will.*

What Are My Coping Mechanisms?

How does he do it? Up at 6:00 a.m. every day, jogs two miles, works until at least 6:00 p.m., spends a lot of time with his family and seems to be involved in all kinds of community affairs. What's the secret? If, indeed, this person is *comfortable* doing all of these things, then we suspect a good deal of it is genetic. One of the many personality traits that seems to be inherited, rather than learned, is energy level. But let's not blame it all on heredity. We have seen many people go from being depressed and apathetic to being full of energy and enthusiasm once they have confronted their own personal bogeyman. Sometimes this does not happen until the mid-40s, and sometimes it does not happen at all. But many of us carry into adulthood all kinds of negative messages that make us afraid of life and people and keep us fearful and stuck. We may have been told that we aren't attractive or that we aren't smart or that we'll never amount to anything. These messages stay with us for a long time. We unconsciously say them to ourselves as adults, and they keep us down. When we see people finally get free of those messages, we see people often bursting with energy.

Nevertheless, we each have a tempo of living that fits us comfortably, and it is important to find that tempo and be at peace with it. Coping mechanisms are a part of that process. Let's go back to our earlier example of the person who had a near-accident on the highway, had an argument at work and then had a flight to New York delayed.

We find him or her sitting at the airport, waiting for the plane. Below are some possible coping mechanisms that person could use.

> Pace up and down, getting angrier and angrier.
> Yell at the ticket agent.
> Take three deep breaths, relax and read the paper.
> Use the time to make a list of things you need to do next week.
> Strike up a conversation with the person next to you.
> Go to the bar and have three stiff drinks.
> Take a tranquilizer.
> Meditate.
> Call a friend you haven't spoken to for a few weeks.

We're sure you can think of many other ways to deal with the stress of the frustration you are feeling. The important thing to remember here is to monitor the effects of your coping mechanisms on that stress escalation curve that we presented earlier. Is what you are doing allowing your body to get back to a normal level of arousal? Or is it escalating your level of arousal even more? In other words, there are *healthy coping mechanisms* and there are *unhealthy coping mechanisms*.

Here are some examples of *healthy* ones:

Moderate Exercise

On a regular basis, this can make you feel vibrant and alive. It will increase the blood flow to your brain and make you more alert, and it even can help to reduce depression.

Meditation Or Biofeedback

These both require that you shut off the "chatter" in your mind for a while, that you listen carefully to what your body is telling you and that you learn to become an expert at willfully quieting your nervous system.

Conflict Resolution

Unless we are hermits, we are bound to have conflicts with the people in our lives. Letting these stay submerged for weeks or months on end produces stress, anger and resentment. If it's bothering you on a regular basis, get it out tactfully and gently. If you have problems doing this, seek competent professional help. Whether it's for your marriage, your business or your children, it will be the best money you've ever spent.

Self-Knowledge

Are you worth enough to yourself to spend some time with yourself? Americans tend to be extroverted more than people in other countries, which is fine, except that sometimes we extroverts don't spend enough, or any, time alone. Time to let our hopes and dreams take shape. Time to look at what makes us happy and what doesn't. Time to *just be* rather than to *do* everything. Get to know yourself.

Here are some examples of *unhealthy coping mechanisms:*

Chemicals

In moderation, alcohol is fine. But chemical abuse and alcoholism are rapidly becoming the number one health problem in

America. Fortunately, the stigma attached to these problems is also rapidly diminishing. Good help is everywhere.

Work Addiction

A lot of us use this to avoid looking at other areas of our lives. "Gee, honey, I'm sorry. I can't talk with you about Jimmy's problems at school. I have to work late again tonight." Too much of a good thing is not good.

Anger/Control

Working myself into a rage about something out of my control is one of the best ways to keep the stress escalation going. The plane is late, and that is it. No matter how angry I get, it won't make the plane appear at the jetway any sooner; but it certainly *will* raise my blood pressure and heart rate, and maybe do even more. Learning to let go of the uncontrollable is perhaps the most subtle, powerful and magnificent way to live a comfortable life.

Avoiding Problems

Sometimes it works; sometimes it's even necessary for a time. Over the long haul, it always backfires. Serious problems do not go away. In fact, what usually happens is that they spill over into other areas of our lives and become so muddled that we can't even identify the problem anymore. Then we're in a real pickle! Is it the carburetor? No, it's plugs. No, it must be the emission control system. No, heck, I don't know what it is anymore. The thing just runs horribly now. What a mess!

Look at your coping mechanisms. Find some new ones if the old ones aren't working for you any longer.

How Do I Take Hold Of My Own Stress?

I've taken a stress assessment of myself, and I think I have some problems to look at. What do I do next? In our clinical practice, we have found that the simpler we keep it, the better. This applies to ourselves as well as to our clients. There is no magical answer outside of ourselves. The magic must come from within. This requires looking at our *lifestyle as a whole*. One very effective system for doing this is shown in Figure 12.3.

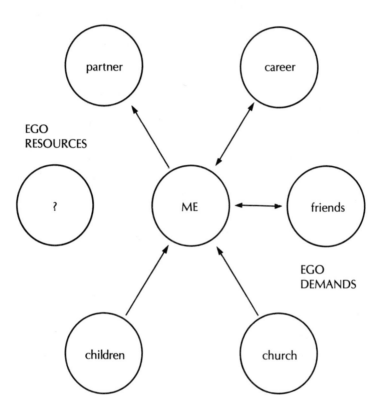

Figure 12.3. My Lifestyle

The inner circle is you. The outer circles are the roles and responsibilities that make up your lifestyle. They are both *ego-resources* and *ego-demands* because they can give us strength and meaning or they can become a drain on us, depending on how they work for us. For example, my career can make me feel useful and competent, or at times it can make me tired and feel useless. My friends can be a source of support and companionship,

or they can be a drain on me if there is too much "take" and not
enough "give."

Do this exercise on a separate sheet of paper. Don't make too
many outer circles. Five should be enough, with perhaps one
unconnected circle to represent a possible new role or activity
that you are thinking about. Connect the inner circles with the
outer ones. The crucial part is to put in arrow-points to show the
flow of energy. In the example above, *at this point in time*, there
is a balanced flow from friends and career *to* me and *from* me.
Church and children seem to be giving me more than I am giving
back. And I feel that I am giving more to my partner than I am
getting back.

This exercise will help you get the big picture for yourself. It
will tell you where your energies are flowing and where you are
drawing energy for yourself. Hopefully, the overall picture will
balance out. In the case where all of the arrows are pointing
outward, with none pointing inward, you are probably dealing
with severe burnout or are heading for it. Keep in mind that this
can be a difficult exercise, too. We may not want to admit that
our job is draining us or that we are overextended and can't
sustain being superwoman or superman much longer.

It also can raise a lot of feelings and questions which, while
frightening, may be the key to better health.

- Am I having trouble with my spouse?
- I had a difficult childhood, so I feel that I must do everything
  for my kids. Am I doing too much?
- I was taught that a "good" person cares for others more than
  himself. Am I being self-destructive by looking after everyone
  but myself, or am I being selfish by thinking about me?

After struggling with this for a number of weeks, one of our
clients said, "You told me that this would help, but all it's done
is stir things up worse than before!" It was only much later,
when she had made some major lifestyle changes, that she was
able to see that it is often painful to look at our lifestyles
honestly and fearlessly. You can't fix your carburetor until you
know it's the carburetor that's broken. Once you know it's

broken, you can get upset about the cost and grieve the dent in your paycheck. You can even get angry. *Then* you can get on with the business of fixing it.

Take some time with this exercise. Learn how to use it as a lifelong tool. File away the old ones for comparison with new ones. Then the next time you feel deluged by all that is going on in your life, you'll be able to sit down and *draw a picture of your stress.*

13

This, Too, Shall Pass (When You're Having A Bad Day)

Part of recovery, perhaps a *very big part*, is about learning how to ride it out, how to weather the storm. In reality, everyone has good days and bad days, good months and bad months, good years and bad years. Our bodies have natural rhythms, the days, months and years have natural rhythms, and our recovery will have natural rhythms.

Sometimes we are having a bad day because we made choices that set us up for a bad day. I chose to stay home from work yesterday because you were hung over, and now I'm swamped at work and you were drunk again when I left this morning, so I'm having a bad day.

But sometimes we're just having a bad day. You know the kind of day we're talking about. The toilet overflows in the morning. The dog throws up on the new carpet. The battery in our car dies. Our secretary calls in sick. And the IRS confuses us with someone else and threatens to seize our bank account. Wow! That's a bad day! There is only one way to handle a day like this — *ride it out.*

Life throws us punches sometimes in threes and sometimes in tens, and sometimes there's no explanation for it and nothing we can do to change it. Are we being tested by God, like Job? Perhaps. Or maybe we're just in a down cycle. It's really hard to know, isn't it? All we can do is wait patiently for a new day and hope for the best.

Learning to accept adversity with dignity, grace and patience is a wonderful part of recovery.

Affirmation:

Sometimes bad things happen. I can ride out the bad times. I have faith and hope that my life will unfold for the best, even when things aren't going well right now. I can trust.

14

Play:
Celebrating Our Spirit
And Our Humanness

Contrary to the serious adult child in many of us, play *is* okay. No, even more than that, play is *essential* to health. Is that clear enough? Because dysfunctional families tend to operate in extremes, play happens in extremes, too. We are either much too serious and *very* uncomfortable with the spontaneous, uninhibited, childlike play of healthy people; or we play in ways that are hurtful and cruel — letting play become an outlet for our hurt and rage. Thus, some of us are deadly serious all the time — working and competitive. Or we do things like tease or tickle or wrestle or verbally spar until someone gets hurt.

Healthy play is a celebration of our spirit and our humanity. Play is what helps us to be creative and to solve problems in new and more efficient ways. Play helps us to keep a solid balance in our lives. And play requires that we have a lot of trust in ourselves and in life, because to play we must *let go* of our tight grip over life for a moment.

Watch healthy little children. When they play, they really get into it! They pretend. They engage in the fanciful. They feel.

They role-play. They get silly. They giggle. You can almost feel their spirits filling the room with joy and laughter and life. That is what true play feels like.

If you are one who engages in *destructive play*, you need to first admit that you are being destructive to self and others. You need to own your offender behavior and to work through the hurt and rage that is beneath it. If you are the *overly serious* type, you need to feel safe enough to let go. You probably also need to get feedback from others about how boring and serious you are. But be sure to find a safe place to get that feedback, because we believe that being overly serious is really about being *afraid*.

Play is life-enhancing. It fills our soul and leaves us rejuvenated and refreshed. If you look at it this way, learning how to let go and really play is certainly worth the risk of some temporary embarrassment.

Problem:

I am too serious and don't play spontaneously, or . . . The "play" I engage in is hurtful and damaging.

Why:

I grew up in a family that didn't value play, or one that used play in hurtful ways. I am scared. Letting go means shame, embarrassment, and loss of control.

Things To Try:

- Tell yourself: "I don't have to do it perfectly all the time."
    "I get tired being so boring all the time."
    "I feel bad that I hurt others when I play."
- Go out and fly a kite, build a sandcastle, walk in the rain without a raincoat, learn one joke and tell it to some friends.
- Ask a friend to go dancing even though you don't know how to dance. Get out on the dance floor and move around.
- Let yourself be silly to blow off steam instead of using your drug or addiction of choice to blow off steam.

- Go to the park and watch children playing. Remember what it was like to be a little child. Celebrate your childhood.
- When you go out with people who laugh and play, stop yourself when you notice that you're judging them. Realize that *they* aren't the unfortunate ones.
- Cultivate a sense of humor in yourself. Start reading the comic strips in the newspaper. Realize that very adult, very competent people read the comic strips because they like to have balance in their lives. Go to a comedy club in your city. Laughter can be contagious.
- Buy some fingerpaints and make a mess on the kitchen table some Saturday afternoon.
- On a slow Wednesday evening sit around the living room and make up stories, with each person adding to the story in more and more outrageous ways.
- Even the most serious people laugh and play now and then.
- When a little sputter of spontaneity pops up out of nowhere from inside of you, notice it. Notice how good it feels. Cherish it. Realize that it *is* possible to build on those moments and expand them.

Affirmation

Play is good. Play is fun. Play makes me whole. I can learn how to play in healthy ways. I can celebrate my spirit and my humanness.

15

On Rejection

Nobody likes to be rejected. It always produces at least *some* shame and fear of abandonment, even in functional people. If I call you Friday evening and ask if you could help me move some furniture tomorrow and you say that you're busy, I will feel disappointed. If I am very attuned to my feelings, I will *feel* just a twinge of rejection, even though I *know* that you still like me. Functional people have enough personal resources and sources of support so this mild rejection is not the end of the world.

But if we are still co-dependent, this mild rejection becomes monumental. We say to ourselves, "Fine! If that's the way she wants to be! I'll show her! Who needs her anyway!" We mope and pout and rage as we try to conceal our deep shame and abandonment feelings. This kind of reaction is not functional.

Whatever two healthy adults are able to give each other is always enough. This is a scary statement because it implies that we can't put all of our eggs into one basket. If I am feeling depleted and have little to give you right now, there's nothing I can

do about it instantly. Maybe over the long haul, but not instantly.
There is no way to avoid all rejection in a relationship.

So what can we do to start dealing with rejection in functional ways?

1. Begin to cultivate a *system* of friends and support so that you have more than one or two people to lean on when you need it.
2. Go easy on yourself. Have a talk with yourself, telling yourself that feeling rejection is part of life and it is not a sign of weakness.
3. *Change* the self-talk you repeat to yourself. Say things like, "I would have liked her to help me move that furniture tomorrow, but she can't. That does not make her a bad person, and it does not make me a bad person."
4. When the rejection is bigger, as when someone we have dated a few times and are beginning to care for says respectfully that he or she can't go out with us anymore, let the pain out. Admit the hurt and embarrassment. Know that everyone experiences this at one time or another. Realize that you are not unique in this respect. Cry. Let yourself be little. Seek support from others. Then let go and move on.

Rejection hurts. Learning to accept a certain amount of it is part of growing up. Take pride in the fact that you are growing up and learning to deal with hurt in a healthy way.

16

Be Kind
To Yourself

Perhaps one of the saddest symptoms of co-dependency is our inability to take care of ourselves. Think about the word. **Care.** Ponder that word. Let all of its nuances of meaning bubble up gently into your conscious mind. Imagine all of the tiny actions that together make up caring. Treating ourselves **with care** is a skill that we have to learn and practice. It actually takes discipline and thought.

There can be some valuable rituals around our self-care, also. Have you had a long, tiring day at work? Are you all stressed out because of the traffic jam downtown? Is your head ringing with noise, your brain on near-overload from too much input all day? Are you on the verge of having a class-one headache? Here is one ritual that works for a friend of ours. We'll describe it as if *you* are doing it, and you can come along with the imagery and feel what it would be like . . .

About halfway to your home, you turn off the loud rock music on the radio and take three deep breaths, imagining the air flowing deeply into your lungs and feeling the air flow out as you exhale. Continue to breathe deeply as you allow the sense of peace and relaxation begin to circulate throughout your entire body. As you pull into your driveway, park your car and walk into your house; put the rest of the world out of your mind and behind you, knowing that you can come back to it any time you choose to. Let your senses speak to you. Notice the late afternoon sunlight filtering through the kitchen window. Feel its warmth. Smell the fragrance of the flowers you bought yesterday as they beckon to you from the dining room table.

As you move toward the stairs, notice even more relaxation flow through your body as you imagine yourself floating luxuriously in a tub of hot water. Go upstairs into the bathroom and begin to fill the tub. Hear the water splashing as it rushes from the spigot. Feel the water's penetrating warmth as you slip into the tub ever so carefully. Let your muscles respond to the warmth as the knots in them slowly unwind and your body goes into a state of deep, deep relaxation. As you do this, notice that all of the stress and cares and traffic and deadlines and conflicts from the day that is now coming to a gentle close are fading into the background, until, slowly but surely, they have disappeared from your present experience.

Isn't that a relaxing thought? *You* can do it, too. But only if you take the time to do it. That's the part that requires discipline. *You can't do it unless you do it!*

Some of the reasons we are *not* kind to ourselves in this way are that . . .

1. We are practicing some addiction or distraction that keeps us from having our feelings, and it also prevents us from being kind to ourselves. For example, I play loud music and stay extemely busy after work so I won't feel lonely, but it also stops me from learning how to relax, and I therefore get a lot of headaches and feel stressed out much of the time.

2. We don't know any other alternatives. We know that drinking is not good for us, so we quit, but we don't know what else to do in its place that might be healthier. If this is the case, we need to educate ourselves and ask lots of questions of other people. This is scary, though, because

we expose our weaknesses when we ask. But it's the only
way to find out, isn't it? So I might say to you, "I've quit
drinking/smoking/compulsive spending/etc., but I'm running out of ways to take care of my feelings/self/stress/
etc. What do *you* do?"
3. Some of us don't believe we have the right to do kind
things for ourselves. We need to stop thinking this way.
This kind of thinking is just a lot of bunk that we picked
up from our family systems.
4. There is someone in our life who doesn't want us to be
kind to ourselves. This person (or persons) might say things
like, "How do you find time to take a long, hot bath when
you have so many chores to do?" Or they might say, "I'm
really angry that you're up there taking a bath when my
shirts aren't all ironed yet." These people need to be educated about the importance of self-care and they should
probably go to treatment for something, too.

Here are some ways that we and others have found to be kind
to ourselves:

1. Take a long hot bath.
2. Buy yourself some fresh flowers for your table or bedroom.
3. Go for a walk in the evening.
4. Write a poem.
5. Meditate.
6. Make a hot cup of tea and listen to some relaxing music.
7. Take a nap.
8. Have lunch at your favorite little restaurant with a good
friend.
9. Build a fire in the fireplace (if you have one and it's cold
outside).
10. Call up a friend if for no other reason than to just say
hello.

17

Journaling:
Make It For You
And Make It Safe

There has been a lot written about journaling over the past 20 years, and we have been keeping our own journals for almost that long. We also recommend journaling to many of our clients. It is an excellent way to begin having a relationship with ourselves for perhaps the first time.

When it comes to *rules* for journaling, we like to stress to our clients that *there are none*. We co-dependents are so good at following rules that we prefer instead to just give some *guidelines* for keeping a journal. These are:

1. *The journal is for you*, not for anyone else to see. It doesn't matter if you're married, living with someone or still living at home with your parents. No one, absolutely no one, has a right to read your journal without your clear, explicit permission. Anyone who does read it without your permission is guilty of the most heinous boundary violation. Your journal is sacred.

At the same time remember we are all human beings and we are all subject to temptation, especially when it comes to reading someone's journal. Therefore, *never* leave it out. If the people around you are especially abusive, intrusive or untrustworthy, then it will be necessary for you to take positive, decisive steps to protect your journal. This means hiding it, locking it up, taking it with you or whatever you need to do to keep it safe. You see, if you don't keep it safe, you won't use it spontaneously. You'll always be writing in it *as if* someone else may read it. You will find yourself editing out your real feelings, hopes, dreams, fantasies and aspirations. In other words, your journal will be pretty worthless.

2. This next suggestion is pretty simple. Write anything in your journal that you'd like. You can make lists. Write poetry. Rage. Be gentle. Cry. Laugh. Daydream. Be silly. Be little. Be big. Work out a fight that you're having with a loved one. Draw pictures. Scribble. Write parts of a novel. Outline lectures. Write imaginary letters to your parents, siblings, people you love or hate. You name it, and it's absolutely, perfectly appropriate for your journal. In fact, some people even put their shopping lists in their journals. Just keep in mind that a journal is all about you, and that anything you do, think, feel, dream or experience *is* you and therefore is appropriate for your journal. Furthermore, as trivial as some of these things may seem, they are not trivial at all. They *are* you. The little things in my life are often the most important. Do you want to trivialize something important about yourself? We didn't think so.

3. How do I start a journal? Go to a store of some kind. Buy a spiral notebook, a looseleaf binder, an actual journal with gold edges and a lock; it doesn't matter. Get something that will become your journal *because you make it so.* See how easy that was? It's a journal because you make it so!

If you have trouble starting your journal, just go to the top of the page, note there the day, date, time, and place. Skip a couple of spaces and begin by answering these questions:

1. Who am I?
2. What do I feel right this moment?
3. What do I like?
4. What am I becoming?
5. What do I want right now in my life?
6. What do I need right now in my life?

7. Who is in my life right now?
8. How do I feel about that?
9. Where am I writing this journal? Describe the room or surroundings.
10. How does my body feel? Am I hot or cold?
11. How do I feel in this particular moment?
12. Am I content? Happy? Euphoric?

18

May God Hold You In The Palm Of His Hand

Sometimes we just need to say a prayer now and then to remind us of our vulnerability and humility and gratitude. Sometimes we need to say a prayer of optimism and good will to lift our spirits. And sometimes a prayer, blessing or wish comes along that supports us, raises our spirits, encourages, lets us be sad and contented at the same time and lets us feel safe and warm.

The Irish Blessing is such a prayer:

> *May the road rise to meet you,*
> *May the wind be always at your back,*
> *May the sun shine warm upon your face,*
> *The rains fall soft upon your fields,*
> *And, until we meet again, may God hold you in the palm of his*
> *hand.*

If this one doesn't do it for you, find one that does. It is part of being nice to ourselves to find a prayer or meditation that has personal meaning. The Serenity Prayer is one such prayer. There are many others. You also can write your own in your personal journal.

PART IV

You Are What
You Think
(Sometimes)

They are able because they think they are able.

Virgil
Aeneid, V, 19 B.C.

19

Perfectionism:
The 20% Mess Up Factor
And The Epitaph Test

The Problem

Why do I keep making mistakes?
Perfectionism.
Pretending we are God.
Making how we feel depend upon what we do.
Believing that people value me because I am near-perfect.

Perfectionism is probably the most common and also one of
the most damaging characteristics of dysfunctional families. When
Dad and/or Mom are perfectionists, we spend our entire childhoods walking on eggshells. We get more and more addicted to
"doing" and trying to please by doing more and more, better and
better because in a perfectionistic family *enough is never enough.*
It's not enough to clean the house once a week. As perfectionists we must clean it so clean and be so obsessed and driven with

how clean it is that we have time for nothing else. We can't enjoy the movie on television because the kids are sitting on the chairs that we just vacuumed. We can't take pride in winning that four-year scholarship to medical school because we didn't quite get the 4.0 gradepoint average that we intended to get or because one other person got a higher grade point average than we did. And we certainly can't tolerate mistakes in ourselves *or* in others. A mistake means that you just didn't *try* hard enough, right? It isn't possible that mistakes are part of being human, is it?

Well, we believe that mistakes *are* a part of being human. And to help ourselves and others overcome the plague of perfectionism, we suggest you try the . . .

20% Mess Up Factor

What is the 20% Mess Up Factor? It's pretty straightforward. Everyone in your particular family, work or friendship system gets to "mess up" 20% of the time without any criticism, shame, blame, belittling, anger, rage or subtle words of correction from you. *This goes for yourself, especially.* So you get to be late 20% of the time, spill your milk 20% of the time, forget to return a phone call 20% of the time, leave the lights on in your car 20% of the time, let your house be dirty 20% of the time, not have dinner ready on schedule 20% of the time, be late for the play or concert 20% of the time and act stupid 20% of the time.

There are many more things we could put on this list, but it would be more meaningful if you made your own list of how you are hard on yourself and others. And if you run into any snags while putting this 20% rule into effect, try the . . .

Epitaph Test

The Epitaph Test goes something like this: Is it important enough to be chiseled onto my headstone after I die? If so, then maybe we should get really upset about it. Think this one through carefully, though. How would you like this carved on your gravestone: "Here lies Bill. On July 1, 1994, he dropped a plateful of roast beef while serving dinner to his boss." Hmmmmmm. Maybe it wasn't all that important.

When your life gets *really* hectic and you *know* that it is only temporary and not a further sign of unmanageability, then shift to the 60% Mess Up Factor. Set priorities and let the least important things slide for a few days. If you let your own emotional needs or those of your children slide before you let the bill-paying or house-cleaning slide, then take a close, hard look at your priorities.

If after trying all of the above, you still feel stuck with perfectionism and flagellation of yourself or others then try this. Make a list of all the good things about yourself. Then make a list of all the good things about your life. Then make a list of all the good things about your lover, partner or best friend. Then make a list of all the good things about each of your children. Do these lists as *perfectly* as you can. See? You have a lot to be thankful for. You have a lot of things that are going right in your life. A lot of your life works.

Perfectionism is just a way for miserable people to deny their misery and then dump it on themselves and others. Find the joy and gratitude and comfort in your life and in those around you, and you will see this ugly perfectionism gradually fade away.

20

When To Let Go And When To Fight

If we had clear answers to this one, we'd be gods. We aren't. No way. But this question is the key to living a peaceful, valuable life. "Serenity to accept the things I cannot change, courage to change the things I can and wisdom to know the difference." This is about *wisdom*. It is about *not* being a victim and about *not* being an offender. It is about having healthy power rather than always yielding or always fighting but rarely winning. This is one of the true paradoxes of life.

So rather than telling you how you ought to handle *your* particular test of serenity and letting go versus fighting, we will list here examples of how people have handled this dilemma with successful outcomes. In some cases, two different people will handle the same situation in opposite ways and both strategies worked for them. The ultimate test of this issue is whether it works.

The House And The Divorce

1. A woman we know was in the middle of a legally messy divorce. By all legal, moral, ethical and emotional rights, she was

101

entitled to 100% of the equity in the house. Her attorney told her so, and her friends told her so, her husband's friends told her so and her heart and mind told her so. Because her husband was so manipulative and had so little emotional health, he was able to prolong the negotiations for months and months. It was consuming her time and energy and keeping her from getting on with a new life. She finally called her attorney and told him to give 40% to her husband if he would end the negotiations and get on with it. Five years later she was remarried, had a new job and she and her new husband were able to buy a much better house.

2. A man we know was in the middle of a legally messy divorce. His wife wanted the house, was not entitled to it, and he fought her in court for 18 months. For him, finishing the divorce and truly ending the relationship required that he fight this battle. He did win. The struggle took its toll on all concerned, but when it was over, it was really over for him and he was able to move on with his life.

3. A couple we know had the same battle over the house. They have been fighting the battle for two years. It isn't over. It may never be fully over. Their battle is really about unmet needs from their childhoods, but neither of them is willing to get into therapy to resolve those deeper issues and get on with their lives. They have no friends left. They have little money left. It is questionable whether they will ever recover emotionally from this. It is very sad.

The Moving Company

A friend of ours got an estimate from a moving company. When the move was all over, he had been billed and paid $1500 more than had been estimated. He wrote letters to the company but was stonewalled each time. He considered taking them to court, but finally realized it would cost him much more in time and money than the amount of the bill. He let go of it and chalked it up to his own error in paying the last bill before adding up all of the interim bills. He did get very angry about it and expressed his anger, but eventually he let go, focusing his energy from anger to more productive pursuits.

Addicted Kids

A woman we know had two teenagers who had become addicted to drugs. She put them both into treatment but they were discharged early for not complying with the program. They continued to use and eventually brought drugs into the house. After months of agony and soul-searching, she asked that they both leave the house and go out into the world on their own. They were 18 and 19 at the time. They left in a fury and did not speak to her for three years. She cried, grieved, almost gave in hundreds of times but stuck to her guns and worked her own recovery program. Three years later the first son appeared at her door, apologized for what had happened, said that he had almost died, had gone into treatment and that he was now sober and holding down a job. She welcomed him with open arms. A year later the second son did almost the identical thing.

Parents

1. A man with whom we worked had all but given up on having any kind of relationship with his parents, who called him crazy for being in therapy and who refused to respect his rights or boundaries as a 45-year-old adult man. As his parents neared death, they contacted him and asked to have a family counseling session with him. He set up the session and they attended, but they spent the whole time blaming him and his therapist for splitting up the family. Within a year they had both died, and their son was left to deal with his feelings in group. He did, finally letting go after expressing deep anger, sorrow, hurt and pain.

2. Another man with whom we worked did the same thing. His parents came into therapy, and they were able to clarify and finish up *enough* of their issues so he could spend *some* time with them during each year. The end result was not 100% satisfactory to either of them, but the compromise worked. Our client had to realize that they would never change as much as he wanted them to and that you can only have as much intimacy with another as they are capable of having with you. Learning to accept *what is there* instead of hopelessly hoping for *what won't be* is a big job.

But it let him let go of them when they died, and he was able to be at peace with them after that.

The Car

A woman we know leased a new car from one of the Big Three automakers. She paid $15,000 for it. Throughout the warranty period, she had a constant flow of mechanical problems. It almost drove her crazy because she was so busy with work and family that she had precious little time to keep taking her car to the dealer for repairs. She accumulated a file a half-inch thick with correspondence to the dealer and the manufacturer, all to no avail. After four years of this fighting and misery, she turned the car back in when the lease was up. She *almost* leased another car, but then looked at the file and realized that she in fact had not won at all. She *bought* her next car instead, comforted by the fact that she could sell it or trade it in if the same thing happened in the future. She lost the battle, but she won the war by giving in.

21

The Myth
Of Permanence

Somewhere between birth and age 21 we get this crazy idea
that someday everything will be permanent. We have an especially
strong belief that this is true if we are Adult Children/Co-de-
pendents. In fact, if we came from a dysfunctional family, this
myth rules our lives. It's sort of like Ponce de Leon searching for
the Fountain of Youth. It doesn't exist, but we go after it with all
our heart and soul anyway.

This search for permanence is actually a normal phase of the
late teens, 20s, even early to mid-30s. But in Adult Children it
becomes a huge, overwhelming, all-consuming obsession. We seek
permanence in our friendships. We seek career permanence. We
seek permanence in our feelings, attitudes and belief systems. We
confuse healthy identity clarification with a much more rigid fear-
driven need to have everything fixed for life. The sad thing is that
this is not possible. Things change. People grow and develop
. . . even after the teen years.

For us Adult Children, finding the balance between wanting
everything to be predictable and permanent and expecting everything to change all the time (no stability at all) is a big challenge.

Sometimes it seems as if we swing wildly between chaos and
boredom. In fact, health actually lies in the middle.
If your issue is the Myth of Permanence, consider some of
these truths:

1. All relationships end.
2. Approximately every ten years healthy adults go
   through a life transition in which belief systems, needs,
   goals and feelings about life can change and evolve,
   sometimes dramatically.
3. A healthy couple together for 40 years, actually will have
   four different relationships over that 40-year period, because relationships change over time.
4. Your best friend today may not be your best friend two
   years from now, especially if you get into recovery and
   she doesn't.
5. Unlike 50 years ago, the company you work for when
   you first get out of high school or college is not likely to
   be the company you work for five years later.
6. We will never find someone who completely understands
   us and who can meet all of our needs.
7. We can never go back to the womb.

Affirmations

*I live in a changing world. I can change and grow and still
be me. I like learning how to adjust to change. It is a challenge
that I can face with confidence, knowing I will not lose myself
in the process. I can say goodbye to the past and be sad while
saying hello to the present and being glad.*

22

Lay Down And Die Or Sue The Bastards

All of us have been victims at one time or another. Even if you came from the rare healthy family, you have been victimized by something. Being a victim means suffering some loss or hurt whether we have control over it or not. If you get the measles and can't go to your big baseball game, you've been victimized by a measles bug. If your house burns down while you're on vacation, you're a victim of the fire. If you get in a car accident and lose the use of your right arm, you're a victim of a car accident.

And then there is the Victim Role. This is something very different. When we have been victimized over and over during our childhoods we very often take on the Victim Role. We don't know it but we wear that role like a crown of thorns, like a cloak of self-righteous indignation, like a mantle of helplessness.

It was not our fault originally because we were children. Children are always the victims of whatever abuse or neglect their parents put on them. Children do not have the power to leave or change the system. But as adults we do have the power to live differently. When we are in our Victim Role, we *believe* that we don't have that power.

The first step in getting out of the Victim Role is to admit that we're in it. What, you ask? How will that help? "I don't want to be a victim! I'm *not* a victim!" we shout and pout. But the truth is that *we can't change what we don't own.* If I don't own that I'm a victim, I'll never be able to change it. So take a look at these two sides of the Victim Role.

Side One Of The Victim Role

This side looks helpless, pitiful and powerless. We whine, complain, feel like we just can't go on. We manipulate others into taking care of us. We get suicidal and depressed. We get very helpless. The paradox is that when we are in this kind of Victim Role, we are extremely powerful and able to get everyone to jump through hoops of fire to take care of us. Think about "Poor Mom," "Poor Dad," "Poor Uncle Jake" or my "Poor Best Friend" who just can't seem to get on with his or her life. It can be *very* powerful and *very* manipulative. In many cases it's simply a matter of our not having learned any other way to be.

What do I need to do or say to embrace this Role? I need to say to myself and to others, "Yes. I *am* a Victim. I have been a Victim for many years!" It's that easy. Once we truly admit it to ourselves and others, we will be able to *do* something about it because our true feelings will empower us.

Side Two Of The Victim Role

This is the side of our Victim that really fools us. This is the side that looks powerful and angry. In fact, it is our rageful, frightened, paranoic side. It is the side of us that wants to "sue the bastards"; but we want to sue *all* of the bastards all of the time and we want to do it *right now.*

We rage, we posture, we spout and puff and blow steam out of our ears. We waste tons of personal energy and resources, including money, trying to make people own up to how they wronged us. We want to extract our pound of flesh. We always want to get even. We demand that we be right. We demand that the world *owes* us a fair deal. And we would *never* admit that we are victims!

Me? A Victim? Me? Not possible!

We're afraid it is *very* possible.

People who are truly powerful in a healthy way know when to fight and when to let go and give in. Knowing this is a part of having a clear identity. When we are still in our Victim Role, we will occasionally win *some* battles, but we will *always* lose the war . . . which in emotional terms means that our resources will be depleted, we will always feel angry and taken advantage of, we will never be able to let go of the little things that go wrong in life and will always have a chip on our shoulders. It also means that we will never get what we really want or need out of life, so will ultimately feel cheated all the time . . . not a pleasant way to live.

To help identify and therefore get out of the Victim Role, ask yourself these questions and write down your answers:

1. How did I get hurt when I was a child?
2. How was I used by others as a child?
3. Who took advantage of me as a child?
4. Who did *not* meet my needs when I was a child?
5. Which of my role models let him or herself be used?
6. Which of my role models used and abused others?
7. How did my role models get *their* needs met?
8. Was I allowed to have any power in my family when I was a child?
9. Who do I *allow* into my life today?
10. Do they respect me?
11. Do I ask for what I want and need?
12. When I don't get what I want or need, do I have other people in my life who can meet at least *some* of my needs?
13. Am I angry at everyone all the time?
14. Am I helpless and depressed most of the time?
15. Do I expect others to read my mind and meet my needs without my having to ask?
16. Do I feel everyone is against me? That life isn't fair?

Most of us did *not choose* the Victim Role. But we *can choose to get out of that role.* Identify whether or not you're in it. Share this information with someone else. Then find new ways to meet your needs and new people to hang around with.

Affirmation

I choose not to be a victim today.

23

I Can
Work This
Out Myself

Yep! A lot of things we *can* work out ourselves. And a lot of things we can't. Somewhere between doing it all by ourselves and clinging to everyone else for every little move that we make, is emotional health. Remember, we will never find balance in our lives by becoming isolated; and we will never find balance in our lives by running around like chickens with our heads cut off, constantly eliciting approval and support for all of our decisions and feelings and behaviors.

Both *isolation and over-dependency* are shame-based behaviors. In our isolation we fear being exposed, we fear admitting weakness to others, we fear being hurt or judged by others and we are arrogant in believing that we do not need others. It feels safer, but it is an illusion of safety, a dangerous safety. In our over-dependency, we show our shame by not being able to trust our own judgment or perceptions or beliefs without the constant approval of others. In fact, many over-dependent people don't really want to know how they should be living when they ask you for advice. They are really just asking for your advice all of the time because

they feel empty inside and need the attention, but don't know
how to get it in more direct, healthy, ways.

So, where *is* the balance? What does it look like? We see it all
the time, all around us. We see it in healthy 12-Step meetings and
we see it in healthy people. It's the AA meeting where you can go,
share your pain and your crisis, unburden yourself of some of your
shame and then leave, knowing that no one is going to take
responsibility for your own life or hover over you but also knowing
that you can come back next week and share some more pain. In
other words, *it is sharing and leveling and caring with a limit on
it. A limit on it.* Sometimes early in recovery this limit feels cold,
calloused and uncaring. But this is how life works in the adult
world. We cannot have someone there 24 hours a day for us. It
just can't be. That was what it was like when we were in our
mother's womb, but that's not what it's like out there in the
world now. But it *is* caring. And week after week, as we share
with the same group year in and year out, we begin to pull out of
that experience the truth that there *are* people out there for us.

We see it in healthy people who share problems with their
friends, ask for pointers or even advice, but then make the final
decisions for themselves; knowing that their friend is healthy, too,
and therefore *not invested in us doing it exactly the way they do it.*
I may share my problem with several different friends, gleaning bits
of wisdom here and experience there, but never getting so invested
in just one friend that I become a burden to them. *That* may sound
calloused and cold, too. But really, it is simply respectful friendship.

It took us a long time to realize that healthy people shared their
lives with others. It took even longer to learn that healthy people
were not about to let us smother them with our problems. It takes
a strong, clear, healthy person to listen to my pain, show that
they can feel what I'm feeling and then go away when we are
through interacting and not carry all of my burdens *for* me. That
kind of friend is golden. And they're out there.

24

You Mean
I Have Choices?

Yes, we all have choices every day, year in and year out. Hundreds, even thousands of them. When we *feel* stuck, we have come to *believe* that we no longer have choices. And it seems the smarter and more educated we are, the deeper the hole of stuckness that we can dig for ourselves.

"I *can't* go back to school because . . . it will be too hard, I'm too busy at work, the kids won't have their milk and cookies after school, my husband or wife won't approve, my father never finished school, I'm too old, etc."

All you have to do is turn it around, take all of the brainpower you're using to say why you *can't* do it, and then come up with as many reasons why you *can* do it. Remember, coming up with reasons why you *can* do something does not mean that you must follow through with it. Take it one step at a time.

I can go back to school because:

- It will be hard, but I've done other difficult things before.
- I can ask my boss for some time off.

- I can teach the kids to make cookies for themselves.
- I don't need my spouse's approval for everything that I do.
- I'm not my father.
- I know someone who graduated from college at the age of 92.

Just for fun, make a list of all the things you would like to do but believe you can't. Then, just for fun, list at least 10 reasons why you *can't* do each of those things. Then, just for fun, make a list of 10 reasons why or how you *could* do each of those things.

See, you only *believe* you're stuck.

Make Your List Here

25

Just Because
You Believe It
Doesn't Make It Real

Albert Ellis made a whole career out of looking at our mistaken belief systems and helping us to change them. In the field of dysfunctional families and addictions, it is our *mistaken* belief systems that very often keep us *stuck*. In fact, mistaken beliefs are a central factor in our addictive denial. In your recovery from Co-dependency/Adult Child pain, remember these . . .

Just because you bought me dinner doesn't mean I have to go to bed with you.

Just because they are our parents doesn't mean we have to stay around and be abused some more.

Just because you're my friend doesn't mean I have to stay up until 1:00 a.m. every other morning talking on the phone to you about your unresolved crisis.

Just because they are my children doesn't mean I have to do everything for them.

Just because I don't want to believe that you're having an affair behind my back doesn't mean that you aren't.

Just because you don't drink every day doesn't mean you're not an alcoholic.

Just because I'm male doesn't mean I can never cry.

Just because you had a bad childhood doesn't mean you have a right to hurt me or cling to me.

Just because I feel it doesn't mean I can act on it.

Just because you're my friend doesn't mean you have to share everything about yourself with me.

Just because we're sexually attracted to each other doesn't mean we're meant for each other.

Just because you have a Ph.D. in psychology doesn't mean you have any insight into yourself or others.

Just because there's a law against it doesn't mean it's wrong.

Just because the "teacher said" doesn't make it true.

Just because we love each other doesn't mean we can't fight and still love.

Just because we have a marriage license doesn't mean we can never change.

Just because we're in love doesn't mean it always has to be such hard work.

Just because you're my good friend now doesn't mean that you will be my good friend next year.

Just because I'm depressed today doesn't mean I have to be depressed tomorrow.

Just because there isn't a law against it doesn't make it right.

"Just because" isn't a good enough reason for anything.

26

The Otters

Once upon a time, eons ago, there was a family of ancient animals who lived in the primordial forest. They were small fur-covered animals who lived on fish from the babbling brooks that meandered through the forest. They were docile, warm-hearted little creatures who wouldn't hurt a flea, except for the food they ate to survive. They cared for their young very diligently and they stayed together in groups for comfort and safety. Because they felt they were so different from the other animals around them, they eventually came to call themselves "The Odders." Actually, they weren't really that odd, but sometimes they felt like that.

For hundreds of years they went about their business of raising their young, hunting for food and building their nests in the forest. And then one day the Chief Odder assembled all of them together solemnly and made a proclamation.

With his black little nose quivering and his whiskers twitching, he said, "Fellow Odders, something is happening to our world. Grave changes are in the wind. The weather is shifting. The forest is changing. Some trees are dying while other new trees are sprouting up everywhere. I fear that if we do not respond to this crisis in our environment, our entire race will be obliterated from the face of the earth."

The eyes of his fellow Odders were riveted to his face, their ears straining to hear his every word. His face grew sad and tired. "And, my fellow Odders, I am growing old and tired. Soon I will become sick and die. Therefore, I am asking two of you to step forward to act as new leaders. And to make sure that some of us survive, we need to have two different kinds of leaders who try to survive in two different parts of the forest. I believe we need to face this challenge by starting two tribes of Odders — and hopefully, one of these tribes will endure."

His words enveloped the assembly of Odders like a heavy dark fog. The thought of dividing up and leaving their friends and relatives was heartbreaking. They all sat in deep silence for a long time as the wisdom of his strategy began to sink in. Over the next few days and weeks, the Odders began the painful process of choosing their two new leaders and separating into two different tribes. Finally, after two months, the members of the two new tribes said their goodbyes, gathered up their young and their belongings and sadly went off to two distant parts of the forest. The first few years were filled with hard work, arguments, fighting and lots of grieving about their loss as each tribe tried to settle into a new life and a new way of surviving. Each tribe had to struggle to find a new identity, to develop new customs and to make it in a rapidly changing world.

After a few years it was clear that they had indeed picked two very different leaders and that they were evolving into two very different kinds of animals. They still looked the same. But the way they lived on the planet was very different.

The leader of one tribe had decided that the only way to survive was to take this business of survival seriously. He and his Advisors developed an ingenious, intricate 10-year Survival Plan. Their young were taught from birth to be hard-working and industrious. They mapped out their territory and made detailed observations of the behavior of their most dangerous predators. They took pride in their organization and adaptability. Their society began to run smoothly and efficiently. They all came to know that their survival was secure.

Young and old alike agreed that they felt good and safe whenever they would hear their leader or one of his advisors say, "You
ought to get over there by that stream today and watch for
wolves," or "You ought to start getting ready for winter" or "You
ought to gather some more food." In fact, they all liked the
direction and structure so much that eventually they came to call
themselves "The Oughtas," which delighted them greatly.

Miles and miles away in a distant part of the forest, the other
tribe was struggling to find an identity of its own. Their leader
had not been able to formulate such a clear plan because there
was a battle going on inside of himself about their Old Ways and
what he felt might be good New Ways. Their Ancestors, the
Odders, had been hard workers, but they had also liked to play
when their work was done. This new leader couldn't quite figure
out how to do it at first. He had the Impulse To Work but also
the Impulse To Play. And he wasn't exactly *disorganized*, but he
wasn't exactly organized, either. Sometimes this was confusing to
the other members of the tribe, but he was such a warm, generous
leader, and he was willing to lead and make difficult decisions
when they had to be made, that they all seemed to be able to
manage anyway.

After many years this leader grew old and died, and everyone
grieved deeply for their loss. Years after that, as they were remem-
bering the Early Days and their First Leader, this tribe realized that
they had something special. In fact, they were like no other species
of animal on earth. They did the day-to-day things that all animals
need to do to survive. They gathered food. They built their nests.
They cared for their young. They still stuck together in their
tribes. But they also had allowed that Impulse To Play to become
a clear, solid part of their identity. To watch them at play day in
and day out was almost mind-boggling. Scurrying around, wrestling
with each other joyfully, scrambling up and down the banks of
streams and rivers, swimming, diving, sliding down snow-covered
hills at breakneck speed, landing uproariously at the bottom in a
pile of fur and feet and whiskers and laughter. To the outside
observer it appeared that their only purpose on earth was to play!

And yet if all they did was play, they wouldn't have survived. It
was *so* clear and *so* confusing! Somehow they were able to weave
a baffling tapestry of work and play into a blur of daily activity

that was almost beyond explanation. Play and silliness and laughter and joy were happening at the same time as the serious job of surviving in the wild. It was a wonder to behold. And when human beings finally started watching them to see what was going on, these humans finally figured out that one of the main reasons they had survived was that they had almost no natural predators. Why? Because their behavior was *seemingly* so erratic and unpredictable that their predators were absolutely confused. Hawks would watch them but could never figure out where they would be next. Wolves watched them but could never figure out where they would be next. None of the other animals could figure them out, so they just gave up and hunted more predictable prey.

Today we call this tribe that came to survive the great changes in the forest The Otters. They continue to live in the forest, going about the very serious work of hunting for food and caring for their young. They continue to play day in and day out, filling their workdays with laughter and joy and spontaneity. And they continue to baffle their predators as they slip and slide and frolic throughout their day.

The other tribe, the Oughtas, did not experience the same joyous fate. They survived for many centuries with their disciplined, structured Survival Plan. But as each new generation was born and matured, their society became more and more structured and disciplined until one day, when it was already too late, they realized that their lives had become *too* structured. And then the inevitable happened. Their forest started to change again. New predators came on the scene. The weather changed again. Their society had become so unwieldy with rules and regulations that they were not able to respond to the changes. Within just seven short generations, the entire tribe of Oughtas had become extinct. The last surviving Oughta, old and near death, carved a message on a giant tree in the forest, warning other animals of their fate. As he drifted into the peaceful calm of death, he prayed that the other tribe had survived.

Deep in the woods, in a far distant forest, you can still find that message carved on that huge old tree. It reads, "We worked too hard. We tried too hard. We couldn't adapt to change. We had too many "oughts.""

PART V

Boundaries: Getting Tricked, Staying Clear

Everyone is bound to assert his rights and resist invasion by others.

Immanuel Kant
Lecture at Konigsberg, 1775

27

Re-enactments: History *Does* Repeat Itself

The concept of **re-enactment** is a tough one to grasp at the grass roots level. Yet when we keep it simple, it's pretty easy to figure out. What it means is that whatever we learned to be or do as children will continue to be acted out in our adult lives until we identify it, have our feelings about it, and then make a decision to change it (if it's something that we *want* to change). In other words, history *does* repeat itself!

So many of us can't see this process working in our adult lives because by the time we're adults, we're running on autopilot — the patterns have become so habitual that we just assume that we do it because we do it. It's sort of like riding a bicycle or driving a car. When we first are learning to do it, we think about every little step and we focus on learning it. We are excited about the new accomplishment. Months later, when it has become a habit, we forget all the effort that went into it and we just do it automatically. *We take it for granted.* With riding a bike or driving a car, it's just as well that we can now take it for granted. Think of how difficult life would be if every time we got into a car to go somewhere, we had to think and talk our way through every step of the process of driving! What a pain *that* would be!

But when it comes to painful patterns of behavior, like choosing abusive people to be around or choosing to act out addictions instead of taking care of our feelings in healthy ways, it would be a real blessing if these patterns had *not* become habits. But they *do* become habits. To help remind us all about this principle of **re-enactment**, we have listed below some examples of these patterns. See if any of them apply to you.

Old And New Abuse

In childhood, Dad was verbally and sometimes physically abusive to Mom and to us kids. I felt *scared*. And because I was a child, I was *helpless* to do anything about it. Children don't have the power to change adults, and they don't have the power to leave home and go out on their own.

Now, as an adult, I get into abusive relationships with friends/lovers/bosses/etc. I feel scared. And because it's still an unidentified re-enactment, I still *believe* that I am helpless to change this pattern in my life. I may *intellectually* understand that it is a childhood pattern, but I don't realize there are several things healthy people do to get out of abusive situations. I don't know I have options such as getting enough support in life so that leaving the abuser is not so frightening; or that I can talk about the abuse with others; or that I can admit I need to learn new behaviors and that it's okay to ask for help in learning those new behaviors.

Sick To My Stomach

When Dad and Mom fought late at night, I'd lie in bed with knots in my stomach, straining to hear what was going on; afraid that they would hurt each other or leave me.

Now, as an adult, I stay up late at night, don't get enough sleep and am easily frightened by normal noises in the house, but I don't know why.

Medicating Feelings

When I felt sad and blue as a child, Dad and Mom would buy me something, feed me something, give me some medication or distract me somehow instead of letting me feel my sadness.

Now, as an adult, whenever I feel sad and blue, I also get confused and panicky. Then I buy myself something, eat something, take some medication or desperately distract myself. So I never finish with my sadness. I find that I *can't heal.*

Perfectionism

As a child, I could never seem to do anything right. I could never please Dad or Mom or both. They picked at me constantly for the littlest things. I tried and tried and tried, but to no avail. I'm still trying, but it's still never enough.

Now as an adult, I am *very* critical of myself and others. I pick at my kids constantly. I tear myself down. I have very low self-esteem. But I don't know why.

Choosing Men

When I was a girl growing up in my family, Dad wasn't around very much. When he was, he wasn't emotionally available because he was always busy doing something else.

Now, as an adult, I find it confusing and very painful to be in relationships with men. I am attracted to much older men, too, but I don't know why.

Choosing Women

When I was a boy growing up in my family, Mom used to sit
up late at night talking to me about her broken dreams, her fears
about her marriage and her fantasies about the future. I felt
useful, needed, important, helpful, powerful and very close to
Mom. I worried about her, tried to make her happy, tried to offer
suggestions about how she could live a better life.

Now, as an adult, I get into relationships with women who are
unhappy or lost or being abused or neglected by someone else and
who are perhaps in love with someone else when I wish they were
in love with me. Or I fall in love with women who use me, neglect
me, cheat on me, manipulate me and lie to me. But I don't know
why. I had such a "good" relationship with my mom.

Handling Conflict

My parents used to yell and scream and break things when I was
growing up. It scared me a lot.

Now as an adult, I hate conflict so much that I'd do anything
to avoid it, including smiling when I'm hurt or angry, always giving
in to everyone else, or getting an ulcer. Every now and then, I
explode and rage. Or I get into extremely high conflict relationships where I fight all the time, hurt those around me and feel
terribly guilty.

Anger

My parents *never* got angry when I was a child. They got angry
but never showed it, actually. They always smiled, but sometimes
they ground their teeth down doing it.

Now as an adult, I am very afraid of anger, both mine and that
of others. Or I get angry all the time because I can see that Dad's
and Mom's way wasn't very healthy. But I get worn out being
angry *all* the time, and so do those around me.

Being Special

I was very special as a child. I was the "light of my parents' life." I was the "apple of Dad's eye." I was everything Mom ever wanted. Well, yes, I was a little spoiled, but I'd rather be spoiled a little than be abused.

Now as an adult, I can't find happiness anywhere. I can't find friends or lovers who can give me what I really want in a relationship. Sometimes I feel like everyone else is so dumb! There must be *someone* out there who can love me the way that I want. Isn't there?

Being Spoiled

As a child, I was lucky. I never had to take out the garbage, make my own lunch, feed the dog, clean my room, vacuum the house, mow the lawn or get the mail.

Now, as an adult, I don't know how to take care of myself. I keep falling in love with people who will take care of me, but then I don't respect them. I either wind up abusing or neglecting them, or they wind up leaving me; but I don't know why.

Seeing Ourselves

Write down an area of your life in which you're having some difficulty. Then see if you can discover how it might be a re-enactment of a childhood pattern. If you're in a strong and courageous mood, you might even ask a friend for some feedback or help on this. Very often it's easier for someone else to see our patterns than it is for us.

28

Abused By
An Eyebrow

For some of us, it's easy to identify when we've been abused by someone who hits us, screams at us, calls us names, criticizes us or lies to us. But for many it is not so easy to identify *nonverbal abuse*. We must regularly remind ourselves that at least 80% of the emotional communication between two people is done non-verbally. Yes, 80%. If I look at you and appear to be bored, lost, distant or detached; and then as I speak, I speak in a flat mono-tone; and then I say, "I am very excited to be in love with you and I care about you very much," the real message is just the opposite. I can say, "I love you," and really mean I hate you or I am afraid to love you or I am bored or you make me sick or I wish I were someplace else, etc., etc., etc. It's *how* we say it that's most impor-tant. Knowing this, is it any wonder why it is so hard for us to identify when someone is abusing us?

Emotional communication between two people is a marvelous, wondrous, complicated, subtle, sophisticated event. Our body pos-ture, tone of voice, facial features, gestures, phrasing and timing all come into play. When we are listening to someone, our brains are gathering up all of the noverbal language, too. Our brains gather it up and process it, but only at an *unconscious level.* It is our task during recovery to *learn to notice nonverbal gestures and cues* and to make them *conscious.* When we train ourselves to do this we won't feel nearly as crazy around certain people as we do now.

To help you think about this, think about *"the look"* that so many of you got when you were growing up. How did Mom or Dad do **the look**? Did they look down at you and scowl? Did they frown? Did they look back at you in disgust as they walked out of the room? Walking out of the room is abandonment and shaming. Giving **the look** at the same time means that **the look** will quickly mean abandonment and shame. Did they raise an eyebrow while looking shocked and disappointed? If so, that eyebrow will quickly come to mean shock and disappointment when you see it again. In fact, they won't have to express shock verbally anymore after that. All they'll have to do in the future is raise that eyebrow!

Here are some things to notice as you are teaching yourself to *notice* nonverbal language. Look at/for . . .

Eyebrows — up, down, one up, one down.

Eyes and eyelids — wide open, closed, partially closed, looking directly into your eyes, looking at the ceiling or down on the floor, looking to the side of the room.

Mouth — pursed lips, relaxed and open, smiling (smiling while talking about something sad or hurtful?), downturned, sad, sarcastic, haughty, neutral, etc.

Tone of Voice — loud, quiet, soft, angry, seductive, depressed, excited, agitated, sincere, insincere, empty, scared, bluffing, shaky, phony, warm, close, caring, scary, etc.

Body Posture — comfortable, open, accepting, tolerant, aggressive, angry, competitive, contemptuous, nervous, defensive, hiding, tense, rigid, uncomfortable, closed, depressed, calm, relaxed, frightening, threatening, confusing, etc.

There are many others that you can watch. As you watch and learn, make notes in your journal. Have fun with it. Make it like an anthropological investigation. Notice and observe your *own feeling* reactions, too. You *can* learn to consciously perceive nonverbal language.

Affirmation

I can learn to recognize nonverbal communication. I can trust my observations and feelings. I don't have to feel crazy when people say one thing with their words and another thing with their nonverbal language.

29

Some Shaming
Statements To
Watch For

Problem

Sometimes we don't know when we're being shamed because of the confusing nonverbal language used or because we were shamed so often during childhood that we still believe to be shamed is "normal." (It may be normal, but it isn't healthy.)

Below is a sample of some shaming statements and common double-binds that make us feel crazy when they are used on us. See if any are happening to you on a regular basis, note by whom and resolve to set a boundary around it.

*You're _____ (fill in the blank)

dumb	slow	<u>always</u> doing that
clumsy	crazy	<u>never</u> there for me
ugly	too fat	sick
boring	too tall	co-dependent

*Why can't you be more like _____ ?

me	a man
her/him	a woman
sister	Joe
brother	Sue

*You're going to _____ that?

eat	wear
do	say
bring	buy

*Don't even think it!

*Why do you feel *that* way?

*Don't think you can come back here if it doesn't work out.

*I love you/go away.

*C'mon now. You *can't* be angry.

*What did you get this "C" on your report card for?

30

When People Say Inappropriate Or Abusive Things To Me

There are many levels of abuse and inappropriateness, which is why we can get so confused about how to respond. Also, there are many levels of relationships, which often require different responses to the same inappropriateness.

Examples Of Inappropriate Or Abusive Things Said To Me, And Some Possible Replies:

1. "You aren't going to *that* movie, are you?"
   Reply: It is very important to remain calm, matter-of-fact and firm when you say, thoughtfully, "Yes, I am."
2. "You *always* get what you want."
   Reply: "That's not true." Remember to keep eye contact and remain calm.
3. "You were a real brat when you were a child."
   Reply: "Could you be more specific?" "That's not true." "Yes, I was. It was a very painful way to live."
4. "You're really stupid."
   Reply: "That's not true." "I don't like it when you call

135

me names or criticize me." "It hurts me when you say
that." "I need to have you stop criticizing me."
5. "I hate you. I wish I'd never met you."
   Reply: "I'm sorry that you feel that way." "If that's how
   you feel, I need to re-evaluate my commitment to you."
   "Is there something we can do about this?"
6. "If you leave, I'm going to kill myself."
   Reply: "I won't be responsible for your suicide. I'm
   calling 911 to get some help right now."
7. "I have a right to have sex with you anytime I want. I'm
   your spouse."
   Reply: "That's not true."
8. Husband to wife: "Do as you're told. I'm your husband."
   Reply: "I can't live that way."

31

Get An Answering Machine

Problem:

My parents, grown children, friends, lover or others call me on the phone too often, depend on me too much, call me when I am asleep, call me when I have company at the house and won't get off the phone when I tell them that, call me when I want to be alone and I catch myself saying, "Oh, I *should* be *nice* to them."

What I Am Feeling Inside:

Used, angry, tired, taken advantage of, put upon, bored, smothered.

Where Or Why We May Still Be Stuck:

Common wisdom on assertiveness would say that we should first speak directly to the person involved and let them know we need to set a boundary here. We agree with this strategy, in

principle, especially if it is someone for whom we care. But there
are some drawbacks to employing this strategy in *all* situations.
For example, what about the person who doesn't respect the
boundary after we set it? What about the salesperson who calls
when we're taking a nap? What about the friend or relative who
doesn't respect the boundary but with whom we aren't yet ready
to sever the relationship completely?

Many of us get stuck in these situations because we accept the
way it was done in *our* families when we were growing up. When
the phone rang, someone *always* jumped up, an obvious sense of
urgency in their body language, and answered the phone. Through
that hypnotic process of watching our family we learned to do the
same thing and never questioned the wisdom of doing it. What
we were *also* learning in all of this is that we must always respond
to others' *demands* without *ever* checking in with ourselves.

When we look at it this way, it seems outright preposterous. If
you were in the bathtub and someone walked into your house,
into the bathroom, grabbed you by the arm and dragged you
kicking and screaming, stark naked, into your living room, sat you
down on the couch dripping wet, and said, "I have to talk to you
about helping me pick out flowers for my wedding," how would
you *feel*? We can tell you how *we'd feel*! Angry!

Isn't this what happens when we're in the tub and the phone
rings and we race out, stark naked, to answer it? Of course it is.

Telephones are different now, too. We can turn off the ringers
on them when we're asleep, for example, which is something we
couldn't do 20 years ago. Many of us simply haven't kept up with
the implications of the new technology around us.

But we suspect that most of us who have trouble setting
telephone boundaries do so because we have trouble setting boundaries in general. We learned that we don't have the *right to not
answer* the telephone. It *does* stop ringing after a while, you know.
Believe it or not, you *don't have to answer the telephone*. If it's
really important, they'll call back.

Realize that always being *nice* means that you are not being
respectful to yourself *or* to others.

How can this be? Well, think about it. If I sit on the phone
with you for an hour when I really want to be doing something
else, I am going to begin to resent you. I will become secretly

angry and frustrated with you. My stomach will knot up when the phone rings. I'll make funny faces to my roommate when you call, but you won't see me do it because you're at the other end of the phone. We'll make jokes about you and what a pest you are and how dependent you are. And on and on. See? It's much more respectful to just say, "I'm busy right now. I'll call you back tomorrow" or turn off the ringer, don't answer it or better yet, get an answering machine.

Affirmation

I have a right to my own time and space. When I am always nice, I lose myself and lose respect for you and me. I am becoming a respectful person. I can say, "I'll talk to you tomorrow," when I need to.

32

Uninvited Guests

Problem:

It is Thursday evening or Saturday afternoon or Sunday morning. The time doesn't really matter. You want to be alone at this time. Maybe you haven't been alone with your husband or wife for a while. Maybe you haven't spent time with your kids in a while. Maybe you just want to be alone because you want to be alone! The doorbell rings. You notice fear in your upper chest and a little tightening in your stomach. You go to the door and open it.

"Hi!" your friends say with wide grins on their faces and that look of excitement in their eyes. "We were out for a ride and thought we'd stop by. Haven't seen you in a while. How are you?" As they speak, they begin moving toward the open door, as if you have no chance of stopping them, as if you have no doorway to your house, as if you wouldn't dare think of not letting them come in, as if you had no boundaries.

Your stomach knots up some more as the fear turns to mild anger. This is good, because it is the anger that will give you the energy to set a boundary.

How You May Be Feeling:

Scared, angry (not rageful, but the kind of anger that many people call "frustrated" or "irritated"), put upon, shocked, startled, confused.

Some Options:

1. Don't answer the door. After all, you could have been out anyway. If you find yourself saying, "They'll *know* I'm here. Oh, this is *so* embarrassing!" just put those thoughts out of your mind. Unless they have X-ray eyes or are psychics, they truly will *not* know that you're there.

2. Open the door and say hi! But not before you take a deep breath, count to 10, feel and then think. Think about your *own* non-verbal communication. Think about how you want to firmly but tactfully get the message across. And remember that with very pushy people, it is important to speak and act first and firmly, if you can. At the very least, act firmly and clearly very early in the interaction.

For example, Karen opened the door but kept it partially closed. She made solid eye contact with Tom and Sally. They said they wanted to come in for a visit, and she said to them, "Gee, that was really nice of you. I'd love to have you in some other time. This isn't a good time for me. I've been looking forward to this time alone all week. I'll call you when I'm up for a visit. Thanks a lot for stopping by."

3. Maybe they said they just wanted to stop by for a few minutes on their way to someplace else, so you decided to let them in for a brief visit. But then, as sometimes happens, they wound up staying longer and longer. Now what? Let your *anger* come up a little bit to overcome your *fear* of being assertive. People with healthy boundaries are sensitive to subtle social cues; people without boundaries usually are not. Stand up and move toward the door as you say, "Well, I really need to get back to my book (or your hammock or your nap or whatever). It was fun chatting." Make good eye contact and let your body show determination rather

than resignation and defeat. *"Defeated Body Language"* tells bound-aryless people to keep right on staying in your house.

4. What if they still don't leave? Then you have to be more direct. Here it is important to realize that Tom and Sally will feel some hurt and shame, as any human being would. Also realize that by not learning social cues, it is *their* problem, not yours. In this case, look Tom and Sally in the eyes, be clear and direct, *don't* laugh off what you are about to say, and then say, "Tom, Sally, I really need to have you go now. I need some time to myself." Look away, go to the door, open it and wait for them to exit. As they exit your house, it is then usually safe to be pleasant again and say, "It was nice chatting with you. You two have a good day, now."

The Basic Principle: Boundaries Are Learned

My home is my castle. My time is mine to do with as I see fit. I can have a boundary around my house and my time. If I have trouble setting those boundaries, then I may want to do some more work around how those boundaries were violated on a regular basis when I was a child. How are time and space bound-aries violated when we are children? A *very* partial list follows:

1. You have your bedroom door closed and everyone walks in without knocking or asking if it's okay to come in.
2. You want to keep practicing your violin, but Mom or Dad comes in and says, "We're going to the grocery store. You want to come with us, don't you?" You don't, but the way the question is phrased doesn't leave you any room to say no. This form of question is very abusive.
3. You've done all your weekend chores, you're practicing basketball in the driveway because there's one shot that you need to sharpen up before the game on Monday, and Dad comes out and says, "Let's play Around The World." He *could* have asked, "Are you practicing anything in particular?" or "Do you want to play Around The World right now?" which would have left you open to choose a "yes" or "no."

4. Mom doesn't want you to go out on dates because your
   entering adulthood is a threat to her. She needs you more
   than you need her. As you leave the house to get into
   your car, she asks in a plaintive tone with just a touch of
   helplessness and self-pity in her voice, "Oh, dear, before
   you leave, would you just help me hang this picture on
   the wall? I've been waiting all week for your father to do
   it but he hasn't had time. It would make me *so* happy if
   you could do that for me." Yuck! Don't do it.

33

Combating The "Gotcha Syndrome" I: Why Didn't I See That One Coming?

The "Gotcha Syndrome" is very common for us Adult Children. You're having a conversation with someone and they slip in one of those "nasty zingers," but they do it so covertly that you don't even see it until several hours or even days later.

"That's a very nice dress. I saw one just like it at Penney's." (The words here are not necessarily a "zinger." This *could* be a perfectly harmless statement. But let's assume that the tone of voice and subtle facial expression was ever so carefully condescending.)

Later that evening, on your way home, the shame, anger and hurt start bubbling to the surface and you hit yourself in the head and scream, "She got me! What a bitch!"

How did this happen? How could I let her get another one by me? Why don't I see these zingers coming until so much later? First of all, we *do* see them coming and we *do* feel them at the time. Otherwise we wouldn't be feeling them later. What went wrong?

Here's a hypothetical sequence: She zings me. At an unconscious level, I feel it. But I am an adult child, so I don't believe that I have boundaries. I am afraid of rejection. I am afraid of conflict.

She is an "important person" and I am hypnotized by important people. Etc., etc., etc. I shove my unconscious awareness of being zinged even deeper into my unconscious. I smile sweetly, turn a little red, feel lots of shame and continue the conversation. Later, when I get so mad about being "got," I quickly backpedal and start to rationalize and justify her abusive behavior, because she's "important." Or because she's a friend of my good friend. Or whatever. I've done so many mental gymnastics to put this incident away that by the time I see her again, I'm ready for more abuse.

So, what *can* you do? First, let yourself become aware of your own subtle feelings. Stop shoving everything away to protect everyone else. Do you get passive-aggressive like the other person? No, there *is* a better way. As soon as the person zings you and you realize that you've been shamed, say, "Excuse me, I think I'll go over and talk to Pam. I haven't seen her in awhile," and then do just that.

If it's someone with whom you need or want to have a future relationship, then it is necessary to talk to her directly about it. "You know, Susan, that felt sort of shaming. Are you trying to say that my choice of clothes isn't classy enough for you?" And then go on to discuss it with Susan.

But if this is a person who does a lot of this shaming, then they are to be avoided at all costs. There are just too many decent, clear, direct, honest people in the world for us to waste our time hanging on with false hopes to people who can easily hurt and abuse us.

Remember, at some level in our bodies and in our unconscious, we *do* have awareness of being shamed or abused. It is *our job to notice what's going on inside of ourselves.* No one else can do it for us.

34

Combating The "Gotcha Syndrome" II: I'll Think About It And Let You Know Tomorrow

"I'll think about it and let you know tomorrow." Burn this statement into your brain. Say it over and over and over. Write it in your personal log or journal a hundred times a day until you're sick of it. And then say it out loud some more.

When we are first learning to set boundaries, this can be one of our most useful lines of defense. After several years of practice at setting boundaries, this statement should still be used on a regular basis. And look around you. Listen to others. Watch those five percent of the population who came from healthy families. They use it all the time without even blinking an eyelash!

Watch this . . .

"We're having a picnic down at the lake on Saturday. *You want to go, don't you?*" (Notice the highly manipulative phrase structure.) "Gee, thanks. I'll think about it and let you know tomorrow."

"Honey, let's go to Disney World for our next vacation." "That sounds like it might be fun. Let me think about it and we can discuss it tomorrow."

"I'm painting my house on Sunday and everybody's coming over to help. Would you like to join us?" (Notice the use of "everybody." Is Jimmy Carter coming? How about Meryl Streep? Your boss?) "I'll think about it and let you know tomorrow."

"Dad, can I use the car to drive to Lake Tahoe this weekend?" "I'll think about it and let you know tomorrow."

"I need to have a $2,000 raise." "I'll think about it, discuss it with the partners, and let you know next week."

"Will you marry me?" (If you *really* know you want to, say so now. Otherwise, it's best to say . . .) "I'm flattered. I'm touched. I'm scared. I'm excited. And I'll think about it and let you know tomorrow."

"I have a brand new stock offering that I think will make you a lot of money. Do you want to buy 100 shares right now?" "I'll think about it and let you know on Friday."

"That's the lowest price I can give you on that car." "I'll think about it and let you know tomorrow."

"I'd like to make love with you." (But you aren't quite sure.) "I'll think about it and let you know tomorrow."

"Do you think we can afford to add two new rooms onto the house?" "I'll look over the figures and we can discuss it tomorrow."

"Do you want to see a movie Friday night?" "I'm not sure of my schedule. I'll think about it and tell you tomorrow."

35

Confronting Those Crazy Cons (Fool Me Once...)

Problem:

"Never give a sucker an even break." It sounds so calloused. Calloused cons conning crazy co-dependents? No. We co-dependents aren't crazy, and most of the cons we're up against don't even know that what they're doing is abusive. What *does* seem to be true is that, human nature being what it is, we tend to take what we can get from each other until someone yells "*uncle*." We will agree, though, that there *are* calloused cons out there who are dangerous and that they must be dealt with, too. We suggest that you **stop trying to figure out people's motives, stop trying to decide if they're malicious or not and start taking care of yourself!**

The problem for so many of us is that we are *naive*. We just don't know how to spot a con when we see it. And when we do, we are so good at denying our feelings about it (fear, anger, shame, loneliness, etc.) that we have no internal data from which to act.

Some Common Cons:

1. **The Check.** The check is in the mail.
2. **The Call.** I tried to call you yesterday, but you weren't home (when you were home all day).
3. **Being Late.** I'm really sorry I was an hour late. I got tied up in a meeting. It won't happen again. (But it does, over and over.)
4. **The Rager.** I'm sorry I raged at you (or hit you). It won't happen again. Let's make love and forget about it. (But it keeps happening, because the apology is not a true amend. It is just an excuse to set up the next abuse cycle. A true amend requires that the abusive behavior stops.)
5. **Passive-Aggressive.** "I'm not angry," she says, with an innocent, manipulative look on her face and tone in her voice; but she's grinding her teeth and slamming doors.
6. **Mind-Rape.** You don't want to buy *that* car, do you? (Said with a very subtle tone of condescension and implied shock at our obvious stupidity; when, in fact, we *do* want to buy that car, there's nothing cosmically wrong with buying that car; and the real agenda is that *you* don't want me to buy that car for myself because *you* like a different kind of car.)
7. **Sex.** I only want to have sex with you because I love you so much. (Or is it because I'm sexually addicted, can't express feelings any other way, etc.)
8. **Poor Me.** My Little Child was hurt when growing up. That's why I need you to stay home every night and not have a life of your own. You tap into my deep abandonment fears when you go bowling, to 12-Step meetings or to your bridge club one night per week. (It may be true that we were abandoned as a child, but that does not give us license to dominate, manipulate, control, stifle or smother those around us.)
9. **Clinging.** But I have a weak heart; and I've had such a lonely, painful life; and I never got what I wanted from life. I need to call you every day. I need to know every detail of your life. I need to have you spend all your free

time with me. You're my son or daughter. I need you or I won't be able to live anymore. (This con is very dangerous, very damaging and one of the most powerful. Often the "weakest" person in the family system is actually the most powerful and dangerous.)

10. **Numb.** Of course I love you. I just came from a family where we didn't express feelings. You're so sensitive. (i.e., *you're* defective, not me. This is also a very dangerous con, because first we don't get what we need and then we get shamed and blamed for wanting it and not getting it. It makes us feel crazy inside.)

11. **Gossip.** I didn't say that behind your back. If you don't believe me, go ahead and ask them what I said. (With this one, the con is banking on our co-dependent over-trust in others, our naivete and our lack of self-trust. Our gut says it's real, but our dysfunction says, "Shame on me for not trusting him. I don't want to believe that he said that about me. I'm too scared to find out the truth. I don't want to look petty by checking it out, etc., etc., etc." This con works a lot, because we don't honor our feelings enough to take the risk to validate our own truth.)

12. **Drunk Driving.** I would never drive after drinking. (We smell alcohol on her breath, but we want to believe the best about her. After all, we are in love with her. What would it mean if we were in love with someone who wasn't always honest with us? For one thing, it would mean that we were in love with a normal human being.)

13. **Love Making.** I wish you could be more like Tom (or Susan) when we make love. He (or she) just knew how to do it better. (This is more than just a con when I ruthlessly shame you instead of cooperating with you in lovemaking as a sign of our greater cooperative love. It is blaming you for my inability to be direct, honest and forthright. It is a cruel, abusive way to show our own lack of personal integrity.)

14. **The Addict.** I wouldn't have to drink and have affairs if you weren't so . . . (Need we say more about this con?)

15. **You Asked For It?** You asked for it. (No one ever asks for abuse, and it is *always* abuse to be on the receiving end of marital or date rape, hitting, kicking, slapping, punching, verbal or emotional abuse, rage directed at us or rage directed at another person or thing in our presence. The only appropriate place for rage is alone in our parked car, in the woods or other distant place, or in a therapy group where the therapists are highly trained in working with rage.)

16. **You Need To** . . . You need to start jogging. You need to lose weight. You need to make more money. (You name it. If I *ask* you what you think I need to do, then okay. Most of the time, we don't ask. We just get barraged with the advice and control of others who are acting out their co-dependency on us. It's a con to say, "You need to start jogging," because then I can make it about you instead of owning my own feelings. A healthy response would be to say, "I love you very much. This is very hard for me to share with you because I care so much for you. I am worried about you because you aren't getting any exercise, and when you don't, your health really starts to slide.")

There are *many* more cons to which we are all susceptible. Why not start a list in your journal as you begin to identify them in your daily life? And as you work on your list, try to forget about people's motives. Does it really matter whether or not you meant to park your car on my foot? **No.** I'm going to be hurt and angry regardless of your motive, and I will be gun-shy around your car until I am very certain you have changed the way you drive. I can still like you and want to be with you, but I need to take care of my foot from now on, regardless of what you *meant* to do.

Look at what people do. Watch and listen to their non-verbal communication, not so much to their words. Soon, you will be able to spot a con a mile away. And with that new information, you'll be able to go in the other direction and not get hurt.

36

Confronting Those Crazy Cons: What To Do Or Say

Identifying manipulation, deception and dysfunction, unconscious or not, is the first step in taking care of ourselves around others. The next step is to know what to do or say once the con is identified. We'll take the same list from the previous chapter and give you some pointers.

1. **The Check Is In The Mail:** The mail takes a couple of days if it's local and a little longer if not. Mark it on your calendar. When it doesn't arrive, send a certified or registered letter to the person. If it still doesn't arrive, decide whether it's worth it to go after them legally. If so, do it. If not, let go and learn not to loan any more money to this person. Also look and see if you have a habit of getting burned in this way. If so, get some help with it.

2. *I tried to call you yesterday but you weren't home (when you were home all day):* How important is this? Is it a one-time occurrence or does it happen a lot? Either way you can tuck this information away as a sign that you are dealing with someone who is unable to be honest with you, who has problems being direct and who is not trustworthy in some ways. Don't set yourself up to be hurt by trying to change the other person. If it happens a

second time, know that you are dealing with a *pattern* and that you should probably keep your distance from this person. If it is someone for whom you care more than this, *then* talk to them face-to-face, and don't act like a wounded fawn. Simply say something like this: "You know, I need to tell you that I was home all day yesterday. It's okay that you didn't call, but it's not okay that you told me you did when you didn't. It makes me feel crazy and question my own reality. I need to have you refrain from that in the future. Can you do that?"

3. *I'm really sorry I was an hour late. I got tied up in a meeting. It won't happen again. (But it does, over and over):* This is obviously a *pattern.* You need to talk directly to the person *after* deciding what you are willing to do if it doesn't change. If we let others disappoint us like this enough, eventually our self-esteem goes down the drain. So it's probably best to realize that you can't count on this person and you should make dinner plans with someone else for awhile. Tell the other person this, though. The calmer you can be as you say it, the more powerful will be the message.

4. *I'm sorry I raged at you (or hit you). It won't happen again. Let's make love and forget about it. (But it keeps happening.):* This requires immediate action. That it keeps happening means *you* need help in setting boundaries and *your* fear of abandonment is much bigger than you can handle. Get professional help *for yourself!* If it is physical abuse, get legal help as well. There is no excuse for abuse. He or she must stop the abuse for a long time before you'll be able to trust again.

5. *"I'm not angry," she says, with an innocent, manipulative look on her face and tone in her voice; but she's grinding her teeth and slamming doors:* A key issue here is your own reality and sanity. You need to get validation from others that your perceptions are not distorted. Here it is very important to *notice* and *observe* behavior and make a mental note of it. Don't listen to what she says. Notice what she does. The best confrontation here is to share what you notice with her and to focus on your own feelings as you share it.

6. *You don't want to buy that car, do you?:* The reply here is, "Yes, I do."

7. *I only want to have sex with you because I love you so much. (Or is it because I'm sexually addicted, can't express feelings any other way, etc.):* The simple reality here is that if we don't feel like making love with someone, we shouldn't do it. Sex is one small part of love and intimacy. If someone tells you otherwise, let your fear, apprehension and skepticism come to the surface. Share your feelings, such as: "I'm beginning to feel like a 'thing.' " Or, "It doesn't feel right" or "I need more emotional intimacy along with the sex."

8. *My little child was hurt when growing up. That's why I need you to stay home every night and not have a life of your own:* "I understand that this is difficult for you. I also know that if I can't have my own life as well as my life with you, I'll start to resent you. I don't want that to happen. I will be going to my meeting, and I want you to know that I'll be back."

9. *But I have a weak heart; and I've had such a lonely, painful life; and I never got what I wanted from life. I need to call you every day. I need to know every detail of your life, etc.:* Dealing with this kind of powerful manipulation is very touchy to do without support from others. In many cases, some professional help is well worth it. For the record, the only way to deal with someone this powerful is to gently but very firmly set the boundary anyway. Get an answering machine. Determine beforehand how often you want to talk with this person or see them and stick to that without exception. Share your guilt and pain with others. Stand firm.

10. *Of course I love you. I just came from a family where we didn't express feelings. You're so sensitive!:* Well, you may be sensitive, but not expressing feelings is a surefire way to make others feel crazy and abandoned. You can say, "I may be overly sensitive, but I also need to be in a relationship where feelings are expressed. I won't take all the responsibility for what isn't working in this relationship. I'll just own my part."

11. *I didn't say that behind your back. If you don't believe me, go ahead and ask them what I said:* If it's not that important a relationship, write it off. If it is, you may want to validate it by checking it out with others. We strongly caution you to *not make this a habit!* It's a great way for others to get us hooked in to them permanently. The answers we need are actually right inside of us.

The fact that we're even having this kind of a conversation puts the relationship on shaky ground. Check it out if you need to, but if this becomes a pattern at all, get out of the relationship. It's filled with mistrust and triangulation. It isn't healthy.

12. *I would never drive after drinking. (We smell alcohol on her breath, but we want to believe the best about her.):* Just say, "I smell alcohol on your breath. I need to get out of the car and take a cab home."

13. *I wish you could be more like Tom (or Susan) when we make love. He or she just knew how to do it better:* This is so destructive that we can only recommend you get professional help immediately before your self-esteem and the entire relationship are gone.

14. *I wouldn't have to drink and have affairs if you weren't so . . .:* The reply here is, "I will not take responsibility for your addictions. And I will not continue to stay in a relationship where the one I love is killing him/herself with alcohol and hurting me deeply by having affairs. We get serious help right now, or it's over."

15. *You asked for it:* No one ever asks for it. Abuse, date rape, rape, ridicule, physical assault and the like are never appropriate. You need to know that. *None of these is ever appropriate.*

16. *You need to . . . start jogging, lose weight, make more money, etc.:* When others "take our inventory," we need to stop them right there and explain that we won't tolerate it. "When you say that to me, I feel like a child, as if I'm your project. I have problems, but so do you. I need to work on my problems at my own rate. Thank you."

PART VI

Wanting Love
But Tired Of
The Pain

Remembrance and regrets. They, too, are a part of friendship.

Jean Luc Picard (Patrick Stewart)
in *Star Trek: The Next Generation*

37

Is Co-dependency Something New?

We use this quote from Shakespeare to illustrate the fact that what we call co-dependency has been around for a long time. We think the quote stands by itself without further explanation.

Demetrius: Do I entice you? do I speak you fair?
Or, rather, do I not in plainest truth
Tell you, I do not, nor I cannot love you?
Helena: And even for that do I love you the more.
I am your spaniel; and Demetrius,
The more you beat me, I will fawn on you:
Use me but as your spaniel, spurn me, strike me,
Neglect me, lose me; only give me leave,
Unworthy as I am, to follow you.
What worser place can I beg in your love, —
And yet a place of high respect with me, —
Than to be used as you use your dog?

Demetrius: Tempt not too much the hatred of
          my spirit;
          For I am sick when I do look on thee.
  Helena: And I am sick when I look not on you.

From A *Midsummer Night's Dream*
William Shakespeare, circa 1593

38

Caring Without
Being Co-dependent

This is the $64,000 question. There has been such a tidal wave of awareness and recovery groups and theorizing about family dysfunction that many of us have nearly drowned in the process. We're supposed to take care of each other. No, we're supposed to take care of ourselves. We're supposed to belong somewhere. No, we're supposed to set boundaries and look out for Number One. Where is the functionality in all of this?

Whenever there is a new technology or a new theory of living, there is a tendency for society to swing from one extreme to the other. Advanced electronic technology is great for example, but does *everyone* need a fax machine and a cellular car telephone to be okay? Are there times when it makes sense to do things "the old way," like sending a letter by surface mail instead of faxing it? Surely, some of us can wait until we get back home before we make that phone call. Perhaps a car *without* a telephone in it can be a safe haven away from the pressures and deadlines of work and social commitments.

And so it is with the field of co-dependency and family dysfunction, too. The health and functioning which we are all seeking is somewhere between the "old way" that we used to do and the *overplayed* "new way" that many experts espouse. In the area of friendship and love, we find this to be especially true.

The problem is not that many experts have told us to be "selfish" (in the bad sense of the word). It's just that when we try to adjust our lives in a healthier direction, many of us go to the other extreme for awhile before we locate the healthy middle ground. Some of us never find the middle ground; we swing back and forth from one extreme to the other year in and year out.

So, how *do* we care without being co-dependent? How do we have loving, committed relationships without losing our own identity in the process? What does functional caring look like? How does it feel? Rather than saying that our clients should become "selfish" for awhile, we prefer to use the Native American concept of becoming **"self-full."** In our interpretation of this, becoming self-full is the same as reaching the point of **clear identity,** as we discussed in *Adult Children: The Secrets of Dysfunctional Families* (1988).

Having a **clear identity** means that we are at relative peace with ourselves, we are comfortable, natural, genuine, clear, honest without being boundary-less, we know when to stand up for ourselves and when to let go, we like who we are, we like what we do, we like how we live; *and* we have come to this point via a personal search and questioning. In other words, we didn't just fall into this lifestyle by continuing our childhood beliefs and the commands of our parents.

Once we have this **clear identity** the first time, later changes in our identity are much easier to make as we grow older. And it is our clarity of self that allows us to engage in true, healthy **intimacy.** Thus, having identity and self does not make us so selfish that we can't care about others — *it allows us to care about others in a deeper, healthier way.* **Embracing of self allows us to be intimate with others.** This is *not* a contradiction!

How do we care for others without being co-dependent? Without losing our identities in the process? Here are some pointers and examples.

- Over the long haul, there needs to be a balance between what I give and what I receive. If I find myself always "keeping score," then that's a good sign that it's out of balance.

- If I pay attention to my body and my feelings, I will know when I am beginning to care too much for others and not enough for me. If I start to resent you, feel tired, pressured, smothered, etc., then I probably need to take care of me for awhile.
- If I am always getting into relationships where I feel pressured or smothered, then I am either too self-centered or I am picking people who are too dependent. I may need professional help sorting this out if it is *my pattern*.
- Sometimes people around us need more than we do. My spouse might be having a rough time with work or family illness or therapy issues. I may have to give more than I receive for awhile.
- Caring becomes co-dependent when we find ourselves "doing more of the work" than the one for whom we care. If you are having a personal crisis, but *I* am rushing around trying to line up therapists for you, making sure you go to your therapy group, etc., then I am taking away *your* responsibility and making it about *me*. If I let you struggle with your own issues, but *listen, support, encourage, level with you, share my own feelings with you* and *trust that you have the resources within you to make it through this*, then I am probably being healthy.
- Putting as much energy into being with and helping people we hardly know as we put into our close relationships can be okay; but only if our own house is in order. Many of us take care of the entire world while our own feelings and our own children and spouses are hurt, empty, lonely and wounded. We must take care of *first things first*.
- Caring about self takes energy. Caring about our spouse or partner takes energy. Caring for children takes energy. Caring about friends takes energy. Caring for our planet takes energy. There is only so much energy in us. When we give too much of it away, our identity starts to fade and we get out of focus.
- Caring about nobody also takes energy. It depletes us. We feel isolated, lonely and empty. If this is your issue, get some help.
- Caring means that I treat you like a **competent adult**. I don't do things *for* you that you need to do for yourself. I don't drive you to the doctor and go in with you unless it's something really serious and you need the support. (The current television commercial in which the man and woman are

leaving the doctor's office together happily because he doesn't have to have his hemorrhoids removed *does not* qualify as serious enough, in our opinion!)

- As a **competent adult**, you don't want me to try to read your mind and anticipate your every need and want. You will appreciate the considerate things that I do; and I will ask you how you are doing or how your day was. But you won't expect me to pull it out of you like a dentist pulling teeth and you won't want me to hover over you all the time. You will do nice things for me and I for you. We will see these as **gifts**, freely given; and not as things that we demand and manipulate to get.

- Caring is sometimes painful, as when I say, "I notice that you have been drinking a lot, or that you have been struggling with your weight, and I care for you." Or, when we say, "You're only 15. You're clearly depressed or suicidal or addicted. Because I care, I am putting you into treatment."

- Caring is also *detached and intimate* at the same time. "If you have a monkey on your back, you can take it off and let it jump around my living room. But when you go, take the monkey with you." **Functional people care about each other very deeply.** But the caring always includes self. And it includes respect for the right and responsibility of each of us to find our true path. In the Preface to our first book, we called co-dependency the "Chase-Your-Spouse-Around-The-House-With-The-Self-Help-Book-Syndrome." Taking responsibility for another adult's life is not healthy caring.

- I care about you. I can feel your pain or hurt or sadness when I am with you. When I leave, I can let go of it and go about my day. I will think about you now and then. But I will *not* become **consumed** by you.

39

How Do I *End* This Relationship?

This is a very difficult one for many of us. We have been in a relationship for months or years, we have tried to make it better, we have been in couples counseling and nothing seems to work. When you make that decision to get out of a relationship, letting the other person know clearly and cleanly will be the last important act of intimacy and respect that you will do.

Where we get so muddled and confused is that our guilt, distorted loyalty and need to be in control take charge. Our fear of being alone grabs us by the throat and chokes off all reason. As a result, we do all kinds of *cruel* things to our partner, friend or lover. Some of the cruel things we do are . . .

- We say we want out of the relationship then we continue to initiate contact with that person, making them feel crazy and giving them false hope.
- We say that we want to be just friends, even though we know at some level that the other person can't be just friends because they are still madly in love with us or are

deeply dependent on us or both. We know this but we
pretend we don't know it.

- We pretend that when the other person makes up reasons to
see us again it doesn't mean anything and that it's perfectly
fine to meet for that reason. "I need to stop by and pick up
that coffee pot I left before I moved out" may be a legitimate
request. It also may be an unconscious ploy to try to see you
again and start up the relationship.

- Because we don't take care of our loneliness and vulnerability
we have moments of great weakness when we do things like
sleep with a former lover, telling ourselves that this is just
one more time for old times' sake. In fact, doing this is just
one more confusing message to the other person that will
prolong their pain and grieving process.

- After a while, if the other person is especially persistent,
they will continue to call us or just happen to run into us at
the grocery store every other day. Many of us will notice
inside that we are uncomfortable, but we continue to be
unclear about our boundaries.

- In more severe cases, we succumb to threats of self-inflicted
harm on the part of a former friend or lover. We become
emotional hostages in the relationship, which just keeps the
whole thing going.

Ending a relationship is one of the most painful experiences
anyone can have, whether they are on the sending *or* the receiving
end of the process. While each relationship is different, there *are*
some general rules of thumb to keep in mind when ending one.
The first one is that the length and intensity of the relationship
will determine how much energy you put into trying to save it.
Many painful relationships are worth saving, but many are not.
The entire first stage of getting out is really a stage of trying to
make it work. It is only after trying to make it work and seeing it
isn't possible that we are truly ready to end it.

Once you have determined that it is time to end it, and only
you can make that final decision, *then* we suggest you keep the
following pointers in mind.

- Don't say that you want to leave the relationship until you are ready to. Using the threat of leaving as a manipulative tool to get what you want in a relationship is destructive to both of you.
- When you *are* ready to leave, have enough respect for both of you to sit down, face the other person, and tell them directly that you need to leave. Let the other person have their feelings but hold your own ground, too.
- If the other person, after a few of these conversations, refuses to believe that it's over and continues to demand more and more reasons, argues, analyzes, etc., then just simply say *it is a decision that you have made, that it is painful and that you don't think any more contact with the person will do either of you any good.*
- Don't give the other person false hope by initiating contact with them. This is especially important when you are feeling lonely and vulnerable. To initiate contact with this person because you are lonely and vulnerable is cruel to them and only will prolong the agony for both of you.
- Being just friends is one that many of us try out, but unfortunately, it's usually done for very dysfunctional reasons. Many of us do this because we don't want to face our own pain and we don't want to have the normal guilt that anyone has when they end a relationship. *Some* people can pull this one off successfully, but in our experience, very few can do it. Watch out for this one.
- *Do not* have sexual contact with a former lover once the relationship is over. Realize that when you feel like doing this, you need to get back to your recovery or support system and get emotional nurturing in healthy ways. Sexualizing our loneliness is always dangerous.
- While it is okay and even respectful to "let someone down easy" by having occasional contact with them after it is over, it is essential that if you choose to do this, you are very clear about your new boundaries. Don't let the relationship become sexual again during this time, don't let the other person have intimate details of your personal life and don't initiate contact yourself. The really hard part about this is that *if it's over, it's over!*

- If the other person becomes violent, threatens suicide, or is endangering your or someone else's life, seek professional help immediately. The cost of a couple of counseling sessions will be well worth it.

In truth, *all* relationships end. Some because we outgrow each other, some because we move away or just change, and all eventually end because we die (at least in this life). The pain of ending a relationship is therefore a normal, functional part of life. We get in trouble when we start playing God as we try to avoid pain that is inevitable for *all* human beings.

40

What Couples Fight About And How They Resolve It

We could probably write an entire book on this one, but we can't this time around. Besides, when we get into solid recovery, fighting becomes a pretty natural, healthy thing on its own. But *some* examples and strategies do make sense in the context of this book.

First of all, remember that couples (including friends) who *never* fight are in trouble just like couples who fight destructively all the time. Because we are human beings with different needs and wants and values and tastes and beliefs, conflict and therefore fighting *will* occur. In truth, there *are* no couples who don't fight. Some couples just do it so covertly and craftily that we can't see it and they aren't aware of it. If you put any two people together for any reasonable length of time, conflict will arise — and the conflict will either get resolved and the tension will be relieved, or the couple will continue to live in a state of tension.

Second, remember that *anger* is a healthy emotion. It is there to protect our boundaries and give us the energy and drive to make constructive changes in our lives. *Rage* is abusive whether it is directed at a person, an animal, a chair or a car. Rage also can be expressed indirectly by *passive-aggressive* behavior, and this

169

kind of rage can be *extremely* destructive. Rage that is expressed this way is so covert, though, that the person doing it has convinced him/herself that it is perfectly okay; and that in fact, he or she is a "saint." Nothing could be further from the truth.

Third, remember that anger is a *feeling*. The amount or degree that we show our anger needs to be appropriate; and it needs to be expressed in our tone of voice, body posture, facial expressions and gestures. To say with a deadpan face and tone of voice that we are *furious* and *outraged* at another person is inappropriate. But so is raging at them. Somewhere between flat, deadpan expression and abusive rage lies a *whole range* of various levels of anger expression.

For example, if your spouse continuously leaves the car unlocked in parking lots so that things are continuously being stolen from it, it's appropriate to raise your voice, frown, stiffen up a little and say, "This needs to stop! We can't afford it!"

If someone parks their car on your foot, it's appropriate to scream loudly and say, "Hey, you just parked your car on my foot! Get it off! Right now!"

Many people don't like to say that they're angry because they believe it is wrong. This only muddies the water and confuses the heck out of everyone. It also leads to our denying how we really feel. We asked a woman once how she felt about her husband's total lack of support around the house. Her reply was, "I get frustrated." After deeper exploration with her about her feelings, she burst into tears and cried and screamed and said, "I am *so hurt and angry* by how he acts! I can't take it anymore!" There was obviously more than just some frustration here. Believe us, *it is okay to get angry!* We only ask that you be direct, clear and non-abusive with your anger. If you have rage, deal with it in a therapy group or with a therapist one-to-one, *before* talking to the person involved.

With these pointers in mind, let's look at some of the typical things about which people fight and some of the ways they have resolved the conflicts. It is very important to note that these are only examples and that the only successful solution to a conflict is the one that the two of you come up with. The other obvious comment to make here is that there are at least two levels to some of the fights that we have. At the overt level, we are fighting about territory, our "stuff," money, etc. At the covert level, some fights are about deep, unresolved hurts and wounds from child-hood. In this case, deep psychotherapy and couples work will be the only long term solution to the conflict.

Larry, Jill And "The Bathroom"

Larry and Jill were married on a sunny summer afternoon with all of their friends and relatives present to witness the event. Larry moved into Jill's house while they decided how to pool their resources and build a house that met their new lifestyle.

Things were going along swimmingly until one day, about five weeks into their marriage, Larry noticed he was getting "irritat-ed" (angry) by Jill's habit of using his bar of soap in the shower and not returning it to his shelf in the shower. It seemed so piddling that Larry at first didn't even want to mention it to Jill. But each day as he rinsed shampoo out of his hair and, eyes closed, fumbled around to find his bar of soap, he found himself getting angrier and angrier.

Larry's first strategy was to use what he had learned years ago in assertiveness training class. He approached Jill, looked her in the eyes and said that he had something to discuss. She listened and he calmly said, "I would really appreciate it if you would leave my bar of soap on my shelf in the shower." They were both a little uncom-fortable but they got through it. Jill felt it was a reasonable request, and they ended the discussion on a happy note. For the next three days, the soap was right where he had left it the day before and Larry thought to himself that this was a perfect marriage.

On the fourth day, the soap was on a different shelf again and on the fifth day it wasn't even in the shower. Jill had grabbed it in a hurry to wash her hands and had left it in the sink! Larry "lost it." He screamed from inside the shower, "Where's my #$%&*X# soap?!" Jill rushed into the bathroom and they had a horrendous fight. She said that it wasn't important. He felt stupid and shamed and so he said she was inconsiderate and didn't care about him, etc., etc., etc.

After a few tense minutes of silence, fear, hurt, licking of wounds and posturing, Larry and Jill sat down and talked about it in depth. They both quickly realized that the layout of the bathroom wasn't going to work for *either* of them. Jill said she had been angry about his hanging his wet towel over the shower curtain bar and that she felt cramped and tense in that one bathroom when they were trying to get ready in the morning.

Their long-term solution, which we can't all do, was to keep this in mind as a *clear priority* when they built their new house. They talked about a lot of other compromises, like splitting up their time in the bathroom, assigning different parts of the bathroom for each of their own things, etc., but they finally realized none of these solutions would work over the long haul because they both were very territorial when it came to their stuff.

For the year they waited while they built their house, they worked out a compromise. They knew that it just wasn't worth the constant ill-will it caused to let it become a permanent part of their marriage. In their new house, they built a large shower and separate sinks and vanities that were separated by a *large* amount of floor space. They have never had a problem with it since.

Reactions to their story are very interesting. Some people have said there must be something wrong with their marriage because they couldn't compromise or let go of such a small thing. In fact, that they were able to see such a small thing as a potential long-term stressor and were willing to admit that the "child part" of each of them deserved respect, means their relationship is very healthy. When we "try to be adult" all the time, we end up denying the inner feelings and needs that we have. If we do enough of this, the relationship is doomed to failure. What Larry and Jill did was to respect the "child" in each of them, and without a big dose of that on a regular basis, we'd all be in big trouble.

Jack, Frank And The Vacation

Jack and Frank had been friends for many years, and as their careers blossomed in their 30s, they realized they had more money for recreation than they had in the past. At least once every 18 months, they would try to plan a vacation together. But they were getting tired of the camping and backpacking that they had done in their 20s, so they sat down to discuss it.

Jack tended to be a little more enthusiastic and spontaneous about things in general, so he jumped into the conversation by saying, "A friend at work just got back from Ireland, and she said it was the best vacation she'd ever had. Let's go there! We can spend the whole week driving around the Irish countryside. We'll have a ball!"

Frank was swept up in Jack's enthusiasm for a few minutes, but then he noticed some reservations percolating up inside of his gut. Do I really want to go to Ireland, he asked himself. He had actually been thinking of a winter vacation to a warm, sunny, tropical spot. Ireland would be okay, but certainly not his first choice. Right in the middle of all of Jack's continued excitement, Frank stopped, grew silent, motioned to Jack to be still for a moment and then said, "Jack, the thought of going to Ireland sounds great to me, but I had really been thinking more along the lines of Hawaii or Jamaica in the winter. I'm willing to go to Ireland this time if you'd be willing to go to a place of my choice next time, assuming we're still friends and all."

Jack thought for a second and said, "Sure, that's fine with me. You pick the spot next time and that's what we'll do."

And that's what they did.

Cheryl, Ron And The Bank Account

Cheryl and Ron had been together for five years. They owned a house and two cars, both worked, and had two children ages four and two. For the past five years, they had kept one checking account jointly. Ron usually carried cash for his weekly expenses and Cheryl carried the checkbook. They both deposited their paychecks into the one joint account every two weeks. For five years this seemed to work out just fine for them.

But as they entered their sixth year together, they both began to have rumblings of anger, mistrust and fear around the issue of the bank account. With the arrival of their children on the scene their expenses were growing, and at times there wasn't enough to cover everything that they had been buying regularly. Cheryl wanted to spruce up the house and get a couple of pieces of new furniture, while Ron wanted to get a new stereo system and go on a second honeymoon with Cheryl.

It was very important to Cheryl to have a nice house for her growing children, especially since her parents had been pretty poor and her childhood had been painful because of the marital battles that had gone on. Ron, on the other hand, had had a lot of material things when he was growing up, despite the fact that his mother was alcoholic and his father was gone at work most of the time. To Ron, getting away from the house and the daily routines of life was a high priority.

Within a few months Cheryl and Ron were getting into serious, painful and deeply wounding arguments about money. Cheryl would hide money away in small amounts to save up for the house. Ron would ask her if they could take a vacation instead of buying new carpet, and she would just bristle and withdraw and then finally rage at him. For his part, Ron would belittle her for wanting to have such a "boring" life. He said mean, critical things to her, and then he would finally rage back at her. A few months into this scenario, they consulted a financial advisor to get some help in setting up a budget and allocating money for both sets of goals. That felt good for a few weeks, but it didn't take long before they were right back at it again.

They returned to the financial counselor again, believing her previous advice needed to be modified, but it was clear to the counselor that this was much more than a conflict about money. Before they could even get into it again with her, the counselor stopped and said, "Look, I need to say this to you now because it would be unethical for me to continue to take your money for this problem. It feels to me like there are some other issues underneath the money here, and I'm not equipped to handle them." Somehow Cheryl and Ron already knew that, but they had been too frightened and ashamed to admit it to themselves. The counselor's words were exactly what they had unconsciously hoped for.

Ron and Cheryl entered couples' therapy two weeks later. They worked for a very long time, both individually and as a couple, and the pain they dug up was very deep. To Cheryl, money and the nice house it would bring meant escape from the emotional damage she had experienced as a little girl. For Ron, money meant buying the distractions that he needed to stay away from the pain of his alcoholic mother and workaholic father. For both of them, *the money arena became an arena to "prove" that the other one loved them.* When they were done with the bulk of their therapy, they still had problems doing all of the things they wanted to do. They had to save longer for the house and for vacations. But they were able to do it without the pain and nearly destructive fights that they had once had. They were *very* glad for that. And very grateful.

Sally, Emily, "Being On Time" And Alcoholism

Sally and Emily had been friends for about two months when their big conflict arose. They didn't get it resolved satisfactorily for another three years. In fact, the unfolding drama around Emily's always being late for everything and Sally's anger and rage at her chronicles the growth and development of a now-healthy relationship. And it wasn't just Emily's being late all the time that came between them. Sally was a very carefully hidden alcoholic, and her addiction and subsequent recovery also chronicles the unfolding of a healthy relationship.

Two months into their relationship, Sally and Emily were getting ready to go out to the symphony, which was to begin at 8:00 p.m. Sally knew it took 30 minutes to get there and 10 minutes to park the car and get to their seats. Forty minutes total, from door to seats. At 7:20 p.m. Sally shouted upstairs, "Let's go! We're going to be late!" Emily shouted back cheerily, "I'll be right down!" The minutes ticked by painfully as Sally began to pace the floor of the kitchen. Fifteen minutes later Emily bounded down the stairs, threw on her coat and declared, "I'm ready!" They got into the car and pulled away from the house, and then Sally exploded. "Damn it! We're going to miss the first part of the symphony! You *know* they won't let us in until the second movement now. You *always* do this! Why do you *always* do this? What is *wrong* with you?" She was in a rage.

Emily grew silent, steaming quietly, angry and fearful at the same time. "You're so goddamned compulsive about time! I don't know what the big rush was anyway. Didn't it give you some extra time to have your cocktail before we left? I thought maybe a drink or two would mellow you out a little more than this!"

Their pain, fear and angry words hung in the air and then trailed off into a heavy, choking silence until they pulled into the parking garage. Sally turned clumsily toward Emily and said humbly, "I'm sorry," and Emily replied softly "I'm sorry, too." They waited in the lobby until the second movement of the symphony was about to begin and then found their seats. By the beginning of the third movement, they had at least consciously put the dangerous fight out of their minds.

This pattern of love and hate and making up and love and hate and making up continued in the months following. Sometimes Emily would be more on time after that, but she was never quite on time the way Sally would have liked. And Sally, confronted in a somewhat indirect way about her drinking problem became more aware, ashamed and sensitive about her alcohol use. At times she would make some pretty good attempts not to rely on alcohol for her sense of well-being and relaxation, but she never quite got it under control.

As the weeks and months progressed, their relationship began having higher and higher "highs" and lower and lower "lows." They were strapped into a roller-coaster ride that was scarier than anything they had every experienced. Sally's drinking had escalated. Emily was more and more afraid of her, and as her fear heightened, she became quieter and more withdrawn. As she withdrew from Sally's anger and erratic behavior, Sally would get even angrier, because her anger was in response to her very deep fear that Emily would leave the relationship. They were locked into a downward spiral of anger-withdrawal-increased-anger-increased-withdrawal, and all of it was being fueled by shame and fear.

Emily began to reach out for help. She talked to two trusted friends at work and started attending Al-Anon. She did this on her own, without threatening Sally or rubbing her nose in it. When Sally asked her about it, she was honest, but she made it clear that she was doing it for herself because their relationship had become too painful to carry alone. Something about Emily's quiet, respectful determination told Sally that things were changing, that it might actually be safe for her to change as well. Emily had not rattled any sabers in the direction of ending the relationship. Deep inside of her, Sally knew that she had to confront her alcoholism. She called an acquaintance whom she vaguely recalled had a husband who was in AA. She went to her first AA meeting that week, and she hasn't had another drink since.

Their relationship continued to be rough, but the rough spots began to diminish within the first year of Sally's sobriety. They continued to have fights which were scary at times, but those fights became shorter and shorter as the years passed; and they became less frequent and less intense, too.

Three years after their first big fight about Emily being late, they had tickets to a play at a local theater. The play was to begin at 7:30, and they would have to leave by 6:45 to get to their seats on time. At 6:43, Emily bounded down the stairs and announced brightly, "I'm ready!" Sally smiled warmly and replied, "Okay, let's go!"

We have tried to give you some examples of conflict, fighting, and the different ways that people deal with conflict. To wrap up this chapter, we'd like to end with a list of the typical things that human beings fight about. Sometimes it helps to know that you aren't the only one in the world who fights about these things. Normal human beings fight about . . .

1. Money
2. Sex
3. Children
4. In-laws
5. Time together
6. Time apart
7. Turf/territory
8. "Stuff" — mine and yours
9. Soap in the shower
10. Wearing shoes while in the house
11. Neatness
12. Helping around the house
13. What one or the other wears
14. Where to go on vacation
15. What movie to see

16. What to eat
17. What sports to play
18. How we treat each other in public
19. How we treat each other in private
20. Who we spend our time with
21.
22.
23.
24.
25.

Add your own items to our list. Pick the ones that cause you the most difficulty and look beneath the surface to see what's driving a conflict that can't seem to get resolved. Above all, fight clean and fair. Don't name-call, don't rage or pout, do stop and go away for awhile (with the clear intention of coming back) if the fight gets too big, stick with your feelings and avoid blaming and shaming. And remember, if the United States and the Soviet Union can start to settle their differences amicably, then so can the rest of us!

41

Sex

Sex is a form of communication, cooperation, love, expression, bonding, play, intensity, ecstacy, fun, closeness, joy, power, warmth and intimacy. It can be any or all of these things in its healthy form. In its unhealthy form, sex becomes controlling, fearful, angry, empty, "icky," manipulative, crazy, addictive, distancing, using, overwhelming and isolating. We believe sex is one part of intimacy that is very closely tied to spirituality. Great thinkers have spoken of sex as a metaphor for life and death — i.e., an intense physical and emotional and spiritual fusion culminating in orgasm, followed by the necessary end of the sexual interlude and a separating again.

In a healthy relationship sex is comfortable and natural and engaging in sex is freely chosen by both partners each time it happens. It can be passionate one time, silly and playful the next, warm and low-key another time, intense and powerful another. Healthy sex requires very vulnerable and intimate cooperation from each person. It requires honesty, self-knowledge and the willingness to be open and direct. Above all, sex is much more than the coupling of genitals followed by orgasm. Our sexuality is a crucial part of our identities as men and women, and as we said above, it is an important part of our spirituality. Our sexuality is our celebration of who we are and of life. It is our creative energy, our life force, our vitality. Even if we choose to be celibate we are still sexual beings and we still have to come to terms with our sexuality.

To be turned on by another's physical appearance, their body, breasts, penis, hips or vagina is a natural part of being human. If we didn't turn each other on, the species would have vanished eons ago. But *to focus* on another's sexual attributes, seeing them much of the time as just an *object* of sexual stimulation or gratification, is dehumanizing to self, the other and the relationship. It is a key diagnostic feature of sexual addiction.

Somehow, healthy people are able to . . .

1. Be turned on to each other some of the time.
2. Initiate sex some of the time without making the other just a sex object.
3. Respond to sexual advances freely and openly without losing self or feeling like an object or thing.
4. Say no when they don't feel like it and not feel paralyzingly guilty.
5. Have "no" said to them without feeling paralyzingly ashamed or afraid or angry.
6. Tell each other what they want and need in bed and mutually cooperate so that each feels they are getting what they want or need.

When you think about it, a couple's sexual relationship as defined above will be a powerful and accurate index of the overall health of most relationships.

A word of caution is in order here, too. Some couples come in for help and during our interview they say that a lot of other things are going wrong, "but we have terrific sex!" What we usually find is that the terrific sex is either addictive sex, sex used to express anger, rage, dependency and neediness, or some other dysfunctional dynamic. We also find, under closer examination, that the six points noted above are not really present in their sexual relationship. So be careful on this one. It takes two very healthy, mature, clear adults to meet those six criteria.

What does healthy sex look like? With healthy sex, there is no specific answer to this question. Here are some of the things that healthy people prefer to do sexually. *Some* healthy people just do *one* of these, *some* do *all* . . .

- Have sex in the same position most of the time.
- Have one person "on top" most of the time.
- Have oral sex.
- One person likes and receives oral sex and the other doesn't.
- Have sex on the kitchen table.
- Have sex with the lights dimmed.
- Have sex on a beach.
- Have anal sex.
- Use a vibrator.
- Talk "dirty" to each other while making love.
- Give long slow massages.
- Stimulate each other with their hands.
- Masturbate while the other watches or helps.
- Have sex in the morning when they aren't tired.
- Have sex in the evening after they've gone to bed.
- Have sex in the car right before the opera.
- Rub ice on their bodies while they're making love.
- Have intercourse without orgasm.
- Have intercourse with only one person having orgasm.
-
-
-
-
-
-

You or we could add a lot more. Sexual expression is only limited by the needs and wants and creativity of the people involved. More important than the list above, *please* remember that your sexual partner must be your friend, your confidant, your most trusted ally, your lover and pal. We are at our most vulnerable during sexual expression, which means that the little child inside of us is right there, open, free and spontaneous — or scared, ashamed, hurt and angry. If our little child feels safe to come out with our partner, our sexual parts will work just fine.

42

Breaking Out
Of The Owe/
Pay Syndrome

In *Adult Children: The Secrets of Dysfunctional Families,* we wrote of several problems specific to the intimacy patterns of adult children. One of these is what we call *The Owe/Pay Syndrome.* Put simply, we get into The Owe/Pay Syndrome when we let our intimate relationships become something like a financial transaction at our local bank. It all happens so unconsciously, too, that we don't mean any harm by it; and the people with whom we fall in love or with whom we become friends don't mean any harm, either. Yet, *it is an extremely destructive transaction.*

It goes something like this. I'll paint your house, fix your plumbing, sew your jacket, cook you a big meal, babysit your children, counsel you about your painful love affair with someone else, you name it. *Then,* you'll *owe* me something. I won't be very clear about what that something is, but it will be something like *love, sex, friendship, time with you* and so on. I will unconsciously look for ways to help you. Like a heat-seeking missile or a metal-detector in an airport, an alarm will go off inside of me every time I spot a chance to help you, and I'll rarely miss the mark.

What happens with you is similar. You'll be vulnerable and needy like me. There will be things that you'd just as soon have someone else do anyway. At first it will feel great to have the help. It will feel like all those shortages from childhood are being filled up all at once. But that part about having to *pay* will get to be a pain. In fact, it also will get to be downright *abusive.* I might *demand* to have sex with you, threatening to leave you completely with a broken toilet or furnace or no meals at all. In which case you give in and decide that occasional sex when you don't want it is better than having no one around at all. Then you do it to me, too. You ask for way too much help. Then you do way too many things for me. I start to feel as if you're trying to buy my love, friendship, loyalty or long-term commitment. I begin to feel used and manipulated, but I also feel terribly guilty. You begin to feel used and manipulated, but also terribly guilty. Pretty soon we have a real mess on our hands.

Why is it such a mess? Because love is always a *gift.* By definition, a gift is something given without strings attached. If strings *are* attached, it is either a *bribe* or a *political favor,* or both. The question is, how do we get out of the **owe/pay syndrome** once we're in it? Do we just tell this person we no longer want them in our life? Well, that will solve the problem temporarily. But by no means will it solve the problem permanently. So here's what you need to do to break out of this problem permanently.

1. **Be Competent.** Determine very carefully in what areas of life you find yourself getting indebted to others, especially in romantic-type relationships. Do you know how to run a washing machine and iron a shirt and cook a meal? If not, you are incompetent and you must learn to do these things or have the money to pay others to do them for you. Can you pump your own gasoline, change a flat tire, fix a leaking faucet and stop a toilet from running? If not, get a book on it, take a class on it or pay others to do it for you.

2. **Be Aware.** Determine carefully how you get others indebted to you. Start to be painfully honest with yourself. Don't do things for others on a regular basis unless they are doing things for *you* on a regular basis; and then *only* if you are both doing them freely and without expectation. The safest way to handle this in the beginning is to keep the relationship free from favors and gifts and

transactions such as these. Notice how you may *seduce* others into helping you by whining, acting helpless or just by the *mere mention* that you are having a problem with the buttons on your coat or the faucet in your sink (a person learning clear boundaries here will not even mention the problem in the first place).

3. *Take The Relationship's Pulse.* Take a regular inventory of your relationships. As you let your feelings rise to the surface, notice how others may be getting more involved with you than you are with them. Or notice how you are getting more involved with them than they are with you. These are very painful and sometimes scary things to realize, but believe us, it's a heck of a lot easier in the long run to notice them now instead of later. Much later, you will be so entangled with the other person that it will *really* be hard for both you and them to get untangled.

4. *Stay Connected.* Make sure you are maintaining all of the other relationships in your life, especially when you find yourself getting very close to one person, friend *or* lover. Any relationship which requires that you give up the rest of your life is a dangerous relationship, a dependent relationship, and has the potential to become an abusive relationship as well. This will be perhaps the most difficult aspect of your giving up the *owe/pay syndrome,* because we want so much to be able to *fuse* with another, like going back to the womb. But it *never* works!

5. *If You Must Get Out.* If you currently are stuck in an *owe/ pay* relationship and want to change it, it is possible that the relationship will not survive. Know this beforehand. Be prepared for some pain, including lots of unhealthy or neurotic guilt. You can try all the stuff you learned in assertiveness training and communication skills class, especially as you tell the other person what's going on. But no amount of practice or training will help you with the pain and the guilt and the fear of abandonment. Nonetheless if you maintain your other relationships, keep going to your 12-Step groups and your therapy group or whatever, you *will* get through it. The pain you experience will serve as a very potent and important reminder in the future that it is best to be straight, up front, clean and self-reliant as you get into new love relationships or friendships — and that it is never okay to feel you owe someone something, that they owe you something, or that

you're going to make them pay. As soon as *any* of these feelings come up, do something to take care of them *immediately.*

6. **It Will Get Better.** Remember, old patterns are there because we learned them in our families when we were growing up. New patterns can develop, but only if we choose to develop them and are willing to experience the pain of growing up.

43

What Is A
Healthy Friendship I:
It Takes All Kinds

Intimacy. Love. Friendship. Relationships.
These seem to be topics that *everyone* is interested in. And if
you grew up in a dysfunctional family, you're probably downright
obsessed with them. One of the main drawbacks with obsession is
that we get so focused on the topic that we lose our perspective
on the world. Friendship among adult children from dysfunctional
families often becomes a blinding obsession.

How so? The dynamics are fairly simple but very painful. We
have so many shortages from childhood, we have so much fear of
abandonment and rejection, and we therefore have so much need
for control and outright fusion in our relationships, that we find
the social graces and the rewards of simple friendship to be beyond
our grasp. Many of us have such high and unrealistic expectations
for our friendships that it's impossible to meet them. Also, many
of us expect each and every friend we have to be intensely
intimate. We expect each friend to know everything about us, to
share our every need and interest and hope and dream. We expect
them to put us first at all times, to feel what we feel and believe
what we believe. In other words, we expect our friends to *be for*

187

us what our parents *should have been for us* when we were in *early infancy*. This simply isn't possible.

As you start to heal and recover from your childhood wounds and traumas, go easy on yourself and your fellows. Slowly let your mind and your heart open up to new possibilities and new definitions of friendship. There are currently 5.5 billion people on earth, and quite a few of them could be your friends, but only if you start to redefine what it means to be a friend. So let's begin.

Friends are here for us to provide *companionship* so that we are not alone in the world. They are here to *share* parts of ourselves. They help to *validate* who we are by having things in common with us. They help us to *see ourselves* by acting as mirrors for us, reflecting back to us who we are and how we come across to others. Friends meet some of our needs for warmth, touch, intellectual stimulation, recreation, emotional security and spirituality. There are so many things that friends do for us. But you know, with all of these needs to meet, it isn't surprising to see that it is impossible for only one or two people to meet all of our needs. Yet so many of us expect one or two people to do exactly that!

In truth, healthy, functional people have many different kinds of friends who meet many different needs. Not hundreds of friends. Not even scores of friends. But different friends who meet different needs. Healthy people have a couple of very close friends who meet several needs on a regular basis. Then they have friends who are less close overall, but who may meet specific needs quite well.

This next level of friendship might include a tennis partner, someone who likes the same kinds of movies that I do or someone with whom I can share my joys and sorrows as a parent. I may have another friend who likes computers as I do or who enjoys photography. I may see some of these people only two or three times a year or I may see them once a month. We share what we have in common, but we don't share a lot of other, more personal things about ourselves. We don't have a burning need to share deeper things, but what we do share is rewarding, fun and comfortable.

We can have other kinds of relationships, too. Simple acquaintances whom we talk to when we are alone at our child's Christmas play, or people we might have lunch with when we are at a professional conference, or people at work with whom we share job responsibilities but with whom we share little else. *All* of these different kinds of friendships and relationships are important to our emotional health and sense of well-being, each in their own way. The questions to ask, then, are: *What kinds of friendships do I have? How do they meet my needs?* To help answer these questions, let's look at some of the needs we have and how certain kinds of friends can help to meet them.

Intellectual

These needs can be met by friends with whom we share ideas, theories, facts, data, concepts and the like. I have a friend who likes to talk about astrophysics. I have another friend with whom I discuss world politics. And another who likes to analyze movies. We can spend an entire evening discussing these things and the interchange of ideas is stimulating, challenging and fulfilling for both of us.

Recreational

I have a friend with whom I play tennis, checkers, bowling, soccer, you name it. We don't necessarily share much else in common, nor do we have to. We may even be on opposite ends of the political continuum. We share recreation.

Emotional

This includes our need for emotional closeness and sharing, emotional intimacy, sharing of feelings and personal things about ourselves; giving and receiving validation of each other; sharing of hopes, dreams, problems, sorrows and joys. Even these more intimate needs can be met in part by people who are not our most intimate friends. We see this happening in healthy 12-Step groups, where we share personal things about ourselves but in a safe, limited way. Of course, our deepest emotional needs are most often met by our closest friends, our partner, lover or spouse.

Social

These needs include simple social interaction, going to parties or get-togethers, small talk, and the easy, less intense give-and-take that so many of us from dysfunctional families have such a hard time with.

Sexual

These needs can only truly be met in a healthy way if we view sexuality as one aspect of emotional and spiritual intimacy. And they can only be met in healthy ways if we have already learned how to negotiate emotional and social intimacy with others. If you can't look your friend in the eye and tell him or her that you love them, or that you are angry when they take your "stuff" and don't return it promptly, how will you ever be able to tell them what you like and don't like in bed?

Spiritual

These needs include sharing our spiritual beliefs with others and sharing common rituals. But even more, it requires that we create a community of open feelings and honesty in which we each agree that we are less powerful than the group and less powerful than something beyond us. It allows us to exist in the presence of the unknowable and the uncontrollable without becoming overwhelmed by the experience.

There are other needs, and you may want to break these down into smaller categories if you wish, but the above list will give you a good start. Remember that it takes all kinds and that we need a balance of all of the above. To truly look at your friendship patterns objectively, you may want to make a list of the people in your life, how much time you *actually* spend with those people and which of your needs are being met by each person in your life.

Name of Person In My Life	Time Spent With Her/ Him	Needs Of Mine Met	Needs I Met In Them

44

What Is A
Healthy Relationship II:
Those *Close* Friendships

In a classroom exercise we used to do a lot with college students, we asked them to generate a long list for the blackboard containing all the rules and regulations and shoulds and oughts that they grew up with and had to follow in order to be accepted in their families when they were children. The students had a lot of fun shouting out all of the rules once someone broke the ice and started.

They'd yell out things like, "I had to get good grades," "Be nice to your little sister," "Take out the garbage," "Go to church regularly," "Don't fight with your brother," "Eat good food," "Do your chores," "Keep your nose clean," "Don't air your dirty laundry in public," etc., etc., etc.

Then when this long list was done, we had them generate a list of requirements they felt they had for their very best friendship, or that their very best friend had for them. It's amazing how hard it is to come up with a long list here, because for very good friends there aren't a lot of rules. Sure, they said things like, "Be trustworthy," "Be honest" and a few more. But by no means were they able to generate a whole blackboard full of shoulds and oughts about friendships.

Rather than trying to define a healthy friendship in some kind
of absolute way, which would be silly to do, we'll just list here
some of the statements we have heard over the years that might
give you a *feel* for how a good friendship might operate:

- Good friends will respect themselves.
- Good friends will take care of themselves.
- In a good friendship, we both will get an equal amount out
  of it *over the long haul.*
- In a good friendship, we both will give an equal amount *over
  the long haul.*
- In a good friendship, we will have some things in common
  and we will be very different in some areas.
- A good friend will *not* always be there for us. If they were, it
  would mean that they had no sense of self.
- We will be able to share some very personal things with a
  good friend.
- We do not have to feel obligated to share everything with a
  good friend.
- A good friend will tell us when we have hurt them, bothered
  them, imposed on them; and we can do the same with them.
- A good friend can tell us when they're worried about us, and
  then they can let go and leave it up to us to handle it unless
  we ask for their help.
- A good friend will not let us get overly dependent on them
  and they would want the same from us.
- We will fight with our good friends; we probably will fight
  seldom with just acquaintances.
- We can cry in front of a good friend, knowing they will not
  run away, *nor* will they try to "swoop in" and rescue, fix, take
  care of, smother or use our vulnerability to justify their
  existence.
- A good friend can say yes.
- A good friend can say no.

45

Ask For What
You Need (They
Aren't Mind Readers)

This one is *so tough*. And, *so easy*. Once you get the hang of
it, that is. The basic problem here is that in dysfunctional families,
it's too scary or it's generally pointless to ask for what we need. We
either get belittled or shamed or criticized for asking, or we ask
but never get what we want. Soon everyone in the family sits
around and just *expects* their needs to be met, and when they
aren't, they feel victimized. Well, you're no longer in that family
now, and you're no longer a child. You don't have to spend lots of
time guessing what Dad or Mom wants and then feel crazy and
bad when you didn't guess correctly. And you don't have to sit and
wish and wait and hope that a mind-reader will enter your life and
meet all of your needs without your asking. You don't even have
to say *this* crazy stuff anymore: "If you loved me, you'd *know* what
I want and need." Nope! Now you can do it differently.

Problem:

Believing that it is wrong, bad or a sign of being unloved if you
have to ask for what you want or need.

Why:

We didn't get to do it or learn it in childhood.

What To Do:

Below are some examples of things that we and our clients have asked for from friends and loved ones over the years.

- "Would you scratch my back right there?"
- "Will you sit and talk to me for a few minutes about this problem I'm having at work?"
- "Would you help me put up these curtains?"
- "I need you to watch the kids while I go to my meeting. Will you do that for me?"
- "I need to start getting to sleep earlier. Will you do that with me?"
- "I need some time alone. Will you go home now, and then we can do something tomorrow?"
- "I like it when you ask me how my day went. Will you do that more often?"
- "I feel scared. Will you hold me a little while?"
- "I feel lonely. Will you stay home tonight and spend some time with me?"
- "I don't know how to decorate my new kitchen. Will you help me with it?"
- "Would you put the newspaper down and listen to me for awhile?"
- "I need you to spend some time talking to me before we make love. Can you do that for me?"

There's one hitch to asking for what we need. A healthy adult always knows that he or she *may not always get it*, and this has to be okay. We can't *make* people give us what we need. Also, people who are *too needy* expect everyone to do everything for them all the time. The only way to know if it's healthy is to keep in mind the *Principle Of Reciprocity*, which states that over the long haul what I give to you balances with what you give to me.

Also remember that in our pain and survivorship from our abusive families, we may ask for things that others *can't* give us. Separateness in relationships is as important as togetherness in relationships, but sometimes out of pain or fear we try to fuse with the ones we love and ask them to be with us all the time and to meet all of our needs. This is not realistic, and it will eventually destroy a relationship.

A healthy person will say, "No, I can't give you that right now, but I love you and care about you and will be back tomorrow to continue our relationship."

But go ahead. Ask for what you need. And remember we need many people in our lives so that if one person can't be there for us at the moment, there will be another person who perhaps can. Go ahead. Take the risk. All you have to lose is the expectation that you and others must be mind-readers. And what a relief it is to let go of *that* myth!

46

How Does This Relationship Feel?

The list below is reprinted from our book *Adult Children: The Secrets of Dysfunctional Families*, because we have received so many comments about how helpful it has been to our clients.

Use it to check out the health of your relationship. If you're feeling any of the feelings in the right hand column on a *regular basis*, your relationship needs immediate attention or professional help. Likewise if you *are not* feeling any of the feelings on the left hand column, then you need to look at that.

Intimacy *(Interdependent)*	*Dysfunctional Relationships* *(Dependent/Isolated)*
whole	desperate
joyful	fearful
competent	anxious
interested	rejected
strong	angry
clear	confused
comfortable	abandoned
peaceful	exhausted
fulfilled	invisible
grateful	controlled
happy	used
excited	manipulated
trusting	empty
alone-ness	lonely
together-ness	identity-less

47

The Error Of Narcissism (They Don't Brag About Their Kids Or Make You Watch Slides Of Their Vacation)

We saw this statement in a magazine advertisement for something a couple of years ago. We don't remember what. It was probably for whiskey or cigarettes, knowing our luck. Anyway, we were struck with the feel behind the statement. Not that we wouldn't brag about our kids or show you slides of our vacation *under certain circumstances*. But that's the point here. *Under certain circumstances*. In other words, some of us who grew up in dysfunctional families, perhaps many of us, never learned any *social intelligence*. We may have tested IQs of 150 but not know how to carry on a conversation for more than five minutes without boring the other person to death. We may not know *what* to share, with *whom*, *where* or *how much*.

A common problem many of us have here is that we go into very minute detail about something that happened to us, like a surgery, a car accident, a painful incident with a lover, etc. We go on and on and on, detail after detail after detail, believing that our listeners are as enthralled with our lives as we are. In truth, a painful reality that we learn as we grow up is that *no one* is as interested in our lives as we are. This is the *Error Of Narcissism* that so many of us make.

The Painful Reality: Nobody Cares!

Of course, others *do* care; but rarely as much as we do. And so it is a part of recovery to learn how to *converse;* how to *talk with* others, *not talk at* others. Talking *at* others is narcissistic and self-centered because we are not being sensitive to our audience at all.

Why didn't we learn how to talk to others without boring them or without being so self-conscious that we can barely get the words out (the flipside of narcissism)? We didn't learn because we didn't have good role models or because we were never encouraged to talk within our family or because Dad and Mom rarely had other adults around the house so we could see them all interacting or because every time we opened our mouths someone criticized or shamed us or because Dad and Mom babied us and did all of our talking *for* us, or because Dad and Mom let us be boring and never gave us any instruction, direction or feedback. This last one has the doubly abusive effect of *making us socially comfortable only at home* so that we never want to grow up and go out into the world and have our own life. Pretty scary, huh?

What We Need To Do:

1. We need to admit, first off, that we are socially inappropriate a lot of the time. We need to get around people who won't put up with our boring conversation. Then, when they begin to back away from us, we need to ask ourselves if it's because of something *we* did (instead of instantly blaming the other person and calling them a "snob" or a "jerk").

2. We need to watch other people who are socially intelligent to see how they converse with each other and with us. We can watch people at parties, at work, on the silver screen in a movie theater, on television, at 12-Step meetings, in our therapy group, you name it. If we don't seem to get anywhere with it this way and we are not already *in* a therapy group, then we need to get

into one soon and state at the beginning that one of our goals is to learn how to converse with other human beings without being boring.

3. We also need to learn how to watch the subtle social cues that others give us (some of us are already way too sensitive to others' cues. In this case, we need to practice sharing things about ourselves in a *safe* place and forget for awhile about what others think). Being sensitive to others' cues is part of the give-and-take of relationship. It's part of the reciprocity.

PART VII

Some
Family
Stuff

All happy families are alike, but every unhappy one
is unhappy in its own way.

Leo Tolstoy
Anna Karenina, I, 1876

48

If You Pity Your Parents, You Have Been Abused By Them

This is difficult for most of us to comprehend. And we must make it very clear that we mean *pity*. We can feel *compassion* for our parents. We can feel *sad* for them. We can *empathize* with them. But if you *pity* your parents, then you've been abused by them.

How can this be? We watch our parents abuse each other. We see Dad hit Mom, and we feel *sorry for* her. But we are children and we have no power to change it.

"If it were me," I say to myself, "I'd leave." But Mom doesn't leave. What's worse, Mom may even enlist us as allies in her victimization by talking *about* Dad when he isn't around. Or Dad, who is constantly criticized by Mom because she came from a male-hate family system, just sits and takes it. He is kind and overly gentle with us, so we find ourselves "liking him better" and feeling sorry for him. What Dad is doing is teaching us to be victims, to just lie down and die when we are being abused by someone else.

Empathy demands that we put ourselves in another's shoes *in a healthy way*. Empathy allows me to do an intervention on my alcoholic wife because, although she will feel shame, embarrassment and hurt, ultimately she does not want to die of alcoholism. I can empathize with her in this way because I have been open to the painful, hurting changes *I* have had to go through, and I have therefore learned that pain and hurt are not always bad.

Pity and sympathy are *condescending*. I *look down* on you. I feel *better* than you. I believe I have all the answers for your life. I also believe if *you* get better, that will somehow be the only way *I* will feel better. In my pity for you, I believe it is my life task to *fix* you, to *rescue* you, to *control* you.

In my empathy for you, I share my feeling reality *with* you. I can relate your pain to pains that I have experienced because I have let myself experience those pains, but I do *not* get *enmeshed* in *your* pain. I can care but remain detached. I can respect your right and responsibility to take care of your own pain. I can comfort you without getting lost in you. Empathy is the ultimate act of intimacy and respect. When you say, "My life is a mess, and my spouse is abusing me," I can say, "Yes, it really feels painful to me, too. What can I do to help?" And then I can judge whether what you ask of me is okay for me or is better left for you to do.

With our *parents*, we must always remember that it was (is) their job to handle their own problems and pain. We are their children. It is *not* our job to take care of or carry our parents' sadness and pain for them. *For them to allow this to happen is abuse to us.* Below is a list of things that parents do to allow us to pity them.

We Pity Parents Who . . .

- Are pitiful.
- Won't take care of themselves.
- Drag us into their sadness.
- Are helpless.
- Seduce us into taking care of them.
- Neglect themselves/each other.
- Abuse themselves/each other.

- Have no healthy power.
- Refuse to grow up.
- Have no friends.
- Are disabled but refuse to adjust to it.
- Are sick but refuse to deal with it in a healthy way.
- Make us their pals.
- Share their problems with us.
- Wallow in their emotions.
- Appear strong on the outside but who we intuitively know are weak on the inside.
- Do too much for us and not enough for themselves.
- Deprive themselves but not us, "the martyrs."
- Let others use them — the "sap," "sucker," "naive one," "sweet guy."
- Manipulate us into feeling sorry for them.
- Use their weakness to have great unhealthy power over everyone.
- Can't admit their weaknesses.
- Hurt others — "the offender."
- Seduce us sexually.
- Refuse to learn social skills — "the dufus."
- Try to be someone they're not.
- Talk but say nothing.
- Embarrass themselves and us in public.

49

What Is A Functional Family?

1. A functional family is one that functions well.
2. The needs of the family members are met. That is, *each* person in the family feels safe and has proper food, medical care, education and so on. Each member feels that they belong and are nurtured. Each member feels worth and value and dignity. Each member gets to be separate, gets to make mistakes without shaming, gets to be playful and have fun, and has spirituality.
3. *All* feelings get expressed in a healthy family, in appropriate ways.
4. Problems that recur get solved.
5. Individual feelings, needs and wants are respected, within limits.
6. The parents in the system are crazy about the kids. They really love them and want them around.
7. Kids are listened to, not lectured at.

8. Parents in a healthy family nurture themselves *and* their own relationship, so the kids have role models for a relationship that is taken seriously and has value.
9. There are clear, flexible boundaries in a functional family.
10. Functional families have members who inherit the predisposition for diseases like alcoholism, depression, Alzheimer's, etc., but they deal with those physical weaknesses differently. They express their feelings about it, they ask for help when it's needed and they each own their own contributions to family problems.
11. In healthy families each member is *accountable* for their actions so other family members do not have to get enmeshed with them.
12. People speak directly to each other instead of gossiping and using each other as messengers between themselves and others in the family.
13. People in a functional family share feelings, confront by noticing rather than by pushing and forcing, and know how to detach from the problems of other family members when it is a problem only that family member can ultimately solve.
14. Advice is given when asked for and when appropriate, but kids also are encouraged to struggle with things on their own, so they won't need parents around all the time to make their way in life.
15. In functional families, people know they must go outside of the family to meet some of their needs. They know that to ask for help when it's needed is a sign of strength and health rather than weakness.
16. Parents in healthy families have friends and colleagues with whom they share their lives and their problems, so the children in the family do not have to carry the burden of solving parents' problems or of being parents' "best buddies."
17.
18.
19.
20.

We all have health inside of us somewhere, even if we do not believe we do. Add to our list as you think of other healthy, functional things in families.

50

From Holiday Horrors To Happy Holy Days

Let's face it. Whether you're Christian, Jewish, Buddhist, Atheist, Moslem or aren't quite sure, the Holiday Season in the United States can be the best of times and the worst of times, to quote a bit of Charles Dickens. We also like what television *Late Night* host David Letterman so wisely said, "The longer I've been alive, the more I see that just about every family's goofy."

A friend of ours was on his way to get some change at the bank early last November and summed it up best, "Oh God, help me! Here come the Holidays again!"

Okay. So what is it about the Holidays that gets us so riled up? Sure, some of it is just the expectation that so many psychologists place on us about how bad it is. But for Adult Children/Codependents, the Holiday Horrors are *very* real. However, they don't have to be. First let's look at some of the things that make the Holidays crazy for so many of us. Some of these include:

1. *The Past Pain.* The Holidays were horribly abusive for us when we were children, so this time of year is a painful reminder of how horrible it was.

2. **The Past Rituals.** We *believe* that we have to keep certain family rituals sacred simply because we didn't have
any choice as children to do it any differently. In other
words, we get maudlin, sentimental and caught in the
part of our Little Child that is still stuck as a Victim.
Think about it. One of the rituals may have been that
everyone went to midnight church service on Christmas
Eve. Another may have been that we all went home
afterward and watched Dad get drunk. We don't do the
last anymore. Maybe we don't have to do the first, either.
How about church the next day? At noon? Or even the
week before or the day after?
3. **The Family Power.** We get around our whole family
system for from one hour to up to two weeks. Recover*ed*,
you say? You can handle it now? It will *help* your family
to have you around them for a few weeks? Balderdash! A
recover*ing* person *knows* that he or she can't be around
unrecovering groups for any length of time, *especially* if
they're family members. A recovering person *knows* that
a family system is more powerful than the individuals in
that system. But this is *so* hard for us to remember, no
matter how much recovery we have done.

We see this every January when clients of ours, who
are therapists and lay people alike, come in saying, "I
almost had a slip" or "I *did* have a slip." It takes only a few
minutes to help them get back on track and realize it was
that painful unrecovering system that contributed signif-
icantly to the slip. We are human. If you get trapped in
the system over the Holidays and get into some deep pain
or acting out, let yourself ask for help. You can get right
back on track and back into recovery, perhaps wise
enough this time to let your fear speak to you next year
around early November.
4. **Think Ahead.** We don't think ahead. Sometime in mid-
October, **think ahead!** Anticipaton is the better part of
happiness and serenity during the Holidays. **Remember!**
If we ignore history, we are doomed to repeat it. **Identify**
what parts of the Holidays have been bad for you. Too
many parties? Too many late evenings baking cookies?

Too many relatives? Too many drinks? Too many bad memories around the old rituals that you have been practicing since childhood? **Write** out a list of these things now, so that when the time comes you can be prepared to set the limits that you need to. And remember that the Holidays are over on January 1. What would happen if you went to sleep during the Holidays and woke up January 1? Would life still go on? Of course it would.

5. **Know Your Limits.** We try to do too much. Some people absolutely *thrive* on all of the socializing during the Holidays. Some people thrive on having hundreds of people in their homes for weekend after weekend. And that's okay, if it's okay for *you*. If it's not okay for you, then just admit that. There is absolutely nothing wrong with having a quiet, intimate Holiday Season. Do as much as *you* want to do, not as much as your family wants you to do.

6. **Beliefs.** We *believe* we have to spend too much — that somehow how much we spend is a direct measure of how much we love our children and friends. We get into debt, we get scared, then we get resentful that they don't appreciate what we've bought them, then we punish them emotionally, then we feel guilty, then we rage at them because we're tired of doing so much, then we feel guilty, then we do too much for them to make up for the guilt, then . . .!

7. **Add Your Own.** There are many more reasons for Holiday Crazies. Figure out what *your* reasons are, share ideas with your recovering friends and family and make some changes.

Okay, you say, those are some of the reasons. Now what are some suggestions for how to do it differently? Here are some suggestions. You don't have to do any of them. Or you may want to do some of them. It's up to you. Why not try:

• Taking the family on a ski trip or a trip to a warm climate for the Holidays.

- Spending two or three hours maximum with the extended family on Christmas Eve and leave it at that.
- Having everyone put their names in a hat, pick names and then each person gets one present from one other person.
- Getting the whole family to work at a homeless shelter or food kitchen on Christmas Day.
- Spending Christmas Day with the extended family, then going on vacation for the rest of the week, returning New Year's Day.
- Starting a 12-Step meeting that specifically meets on Christmas Eve.
- Add your own ideas below.

-

-

-

-

-

Changing Holiday rituals can be one of the most painful, guilt-inducing risks we can take in our recoveries; but after a very short while, it can be one of the most powerful and healing moves we can make on behalf of ourselves and our families. Remember, regardless of your religion, the Holidays have come to mean warmth, love, fellowship, spirituality, recovery and renewal. Hold these principles dear to your heart. Take them seriously. Cherish these values. By doing so you will be showing by your actions and your commitments that you take yourself and your loved ones seriously.

Holiness is a virtue to which we can all aspire. Holiness is damaged by abuse, neglect, stress, hurt feelings, emptiness, anger, emotional dishonesty and fear. We wish Holy Holidays for you and your loved ones!

51

My Kids Don't Help Around The House

"My kids don't help around the house." Have you ever said this? It's pretty common. And it's pretty normal for kids to not particularly *want* to help around the house. The problem is not in the wanting to. The problem is in the doing it. If we're honest with ourselves, there aren't many of us who *want* to clean the house. So why don't they help?

Problem:

My kids don't help around the house.

Why:

Because we don't expect them to.

What? I don't get it. Of course I expect them to. They just don't *do* it! Wrong. Remember, rules are transmitted much more by what we do than by what we say, wish for or dream about. If we don't make it happen it won't happen. If we say, "Would you please clean the bathroom after you're done," and they don't do it; and then we don't do anything to follow up, the expectation we are sending to them is that *they don't have to do it.* Believe it or not, children want structure and expectations set for them. They don't want to be abused, but they do want limits and responsibilities. What happens is that we don't know how to do that.

We see families where this is almost never a problem because the expectation was set when the children were very young and has been followed up ever since. Good habits are just as hard to break as are bad habits. There are some exceptions. Like when our kids are in the age range 13 to 18. Teenagers sometimes have to be more strongly encouraged to help around the house than others. But it is tremendously easier to get a teenager to help if the expectation has been there all along.

But let's say that, like so many of us, you didn't follow through from an early age. Perhaps you were abused with housework and child rearing when you were a child, so you vowed you'd never do that to *your* children when you had them. So you went to the other extreme and spoiled them. The first thing to do is to admit that you have let your kids down. That because of your own painful childhood, you have created a different kind of dysfunction for your kids. This will be difficult to do because we all mean so well when we start down the road of parenthood. But if you can admit that, you can then change it. It's about holding ourselves *accountable.* Once you have done this step, you then need to admit that your life and those of your children have become unmanageable. This is always Step One leading to change. *Then* you can try the following:

1. **Plan.** Sit down with your spouse and discuss how you will present this to the kids. Parents who are not in agreement beforehand set themselves up for big trouble. The kids will work us against each other in their natural attempt to get out of housecleaning.

2. **Meet.** Call a meeting with the kids. Sit down with them and explain that both of you have discussed this and that you are in agreement. Then lay out the plan.

3. **Include.** Include the kids in *part* of the plan. Tell them there are certain things that have to get done each week, and they will have to do some of them. Tell them that this is part of belonging to a family, and that you feel you have made a mistake

in not expecting this in the past. Be genuine, clear, firm and understanding. Let them moan and groan. Agree that doing housework is a pain in the rear. Let them know calmly that you don't like it either. Avoid preaching *at* them.

4. **Write It.** Present a written list of the tasks. This shows, by your *actions*, that you are taking this seriously.

5. **Accountability.** Have some consequences for the tasks — positive ones if they are done, and no positive ones if they are not done. In most cases, if you stick with it, you don't need to punish if the tasks are not done. This should only be used as a last resort.

6. **Try It.** Tell the kids that whatever plan they come up with and agree to will be in place for seven to ten days on a trial basis; and that the plan can be renegotiated as needed, but only if everyone is present.

7. **Follow Through.** Here comes the hard part. Follow through. It is almost impossible to do this without having a checklist that each child uses to record his or her task completion. It's also hard because our natural tendency will be to get sappy and enabling and give in to the whining and complaining and excuses. You know the ones. Like, "Aw, Mom, I didn't start my report until 6:00 p.m. because I was watching TV, and now I don't have enough time to do my chores, but I need the money to go to the dance tomorrow night." Usually one weekend without an allowance will encourage most kids to remember. But the whole process of switching from irresponsible parents and kids to responsible parents and kids can take weeks or months. So if you aren't clear and firm in your own recoveries, you won't be able to follow through.

8. **Get Support.** If you find you can't follow through, get back into therapy, get to some more Co-dependents Anonymous meetings or join a parenting group. Your guilt and fear of rejection by your children will be a powerful force keeping you in a dysfunctional parenting role.

9. **For Example.** Just as an example only, here is a typical list of weekly chores for a 13-year-old:

a. Make bed each morning.
b. Get mail in the afternoon.
c. Feed dog and change dog's water each afternoon.

    d. Take out garbage each evening.

    e. Clean bathroom thoroughly each Saturday.

    f. You may choose to do one other weekly chore for an additional bonus to your allowance.

    g. For each day that you complete all of these tasks by the appointed time without having to be asked you will receive $.75.

    h. If one of these tasks is not done by the appointed time, you will forfeit your allowance for that day.

    i. It is your responsibility to check yourself off on your chart by 8:00 p.m. each day. If you do not, you forfeit your allowance for that day.

Children having to do chores and parents having to follow through with children are rights and responsibilities. Parents and children have rights and responsibilities. It is the parents' responsibility to see to it that children learn responsibility, that they learn to be part of a family and a team, and that they learn the basic skills required to live in the world. This includes skills that will keep the Board of Health away from their apartments when our kids move away from home. No child should be allowed to leave home without knowing how to:

- Iron a shirt or a dress.
- Run a washer and dryer.
- Feed a pet.
- Cook basic meals.
- Make a sandwich.
- Write a check.
- Manage money.
- Clean a toilet.
- Operate a vacuum cleaner.

There are probably more, but if these basic ones aren't learned at home, it means we as parents are guilty of severe neglect. No kidding! We mean it.

52

What To
Expect From
Your Teenagers

No, this is not a chapter about how our teenagers don't help around the house. This is about what it means to be a teenager and what it feels to be a teenager and therefore what you can expect from your kids when they are between the ages of 13 and 20.

First of all, when kids hit puberty, their bodies change. It may not seem like a big deal, but think back to your own teen years. One day we're thinking like adults, the next like children. We get interested in sex. We want to be part of a family, but we want to be part of a peer group even more sometimes. We want to test our own limits and the family limits. We get moody, depressed and angry, then agreeable and joyful. Some parents get very confused by this. If you get overwhelmed by it, do some therapy work about yourself and your own childhood.

Based on years of research on identity development, we have found, along with experts like Erik Erikson, that adolescence is a time of searching, questioning and trying on new hats. It is a time of rebellion in the sense that we were told a lot of stuff as kids and now we have the mature cognitive ability to question it to see if it's all just a myth. The other fact that is crucial here is that teenagers who never question or rebel or test out find it impossible to achieve their own identities as adults.

Likewise, adults who prevent teens from doing this testing prevent their kids from ever growing up. Some parents do this unconsciously for that very reason — "If I keep my kids under my thumb, they'll always be there, they'll never grow up and I'll always 'have' them."

We need to set limits for our teenagers so they feel safe, because they aren't adults yet. When they can go out into the world, pay their own rent and bills and have a good support system, then we can stop setting limits for them. If our kids are in their 20s and still need us to set limits for them, then it is time to stop being their caretakers and let them fall down and make their own mistakes. The teen years are a time of gradually giving more and more freedom, and gradually letting go more and more. It is a period of launching.

Here are some of the normal functional things that teenagers do:

1. They get moody, crabby, defiant and silly at times.
2. They can be cooperative and helpful one day, stubborn and downright rude the next.
3. They may spend minutes or hours in front of the mirror, obsessing about their hair, their skin and their clothes.
4. They may isolate sometimes.
5. They may not want to be seen with you in public.
6. They may experiment with drugs or alcohol.
7. They may experiment with sex.
8. They may share personal things, feelings, conflicts and triumphs with you one week and not the next.
9. They will vacillate in what they are interested in doing when they grow up.
10. They will be fun to have around because they are interested in the world and want to talk about adult things like politics, science and current events.
11. They will fall in and out of love all the time.
12. They will be friends with one person one day and not the next.

13. They will feel immortal at times and will take risks that can be very dangerous.

14. They will make you feel crazy, because one day they will be little and want your advice and support and the next day they will be big and want to handle it on their own or with their peers.

15. They will do a lot of other things like those above, and it is our job as parents to empathize with them — to understand that growing up is hard to do. Their job during the teen years is to get prepared to leave home and be independent, competent, self-sufficient adults.

Having teenagers can be very difficult and straining. It should also be a joyful time. We can watch them grow up and go out into the world and begin to make their own way. We can look forward to having more and more time to ourselves, to moving into the next stage of *our* lives, in which we are again able to focus our energies on ourselves and the greater world outside of the family.

53

How Much
Do I Tell
My Kids?

This is one of the most common questions we are asked when
we do workshops on family. Where is the boundary between adult
and child? How much should we tell them about our personal
struggles, our recoveries, our problems and our relationships? In
our zeal to prevent our kids from going through what we did, we
sometimes go way overboard. When we do this we abuse our
children, we push them away, or we unconsciously enlist their
sympathy and pity so they become enmeshed in our problems.
Kids are supposed to be kids for about 21 years (at least).

It is seduction to draw our children into our adult problems too
much, because kids need us to survive and therefore care about us
very deeply. It is seduction because kids want to be a part of the
family, and hearing the gory details of our lives makes them feel
special and important; and because even if they would rather be
out playing baseball or being with their friends, they will try to
stay home and listen and help, because they need us to be there
for them. We are more powerful than kids, and to include them
in our personal lives too much invites them to share power which
they are not equipped to handle.

Here are some examples of what we mean . . .

Parents Dating:

Karen is 11 years old. Her mom just divorced her dad because it wasn't working out. Mom is beginning to date and she is picking men who always let her down the way Dad did. Karen's mom cries a lot around Karen and tells her what bastards men are. Karen feels real scared when her mom cries so much, and she feels very sad and depressed. She is afraid to leave her mom at home alone. And she is beginning to learn to hate men but to want to be around them all the time, just like Mom.

Vickie's mom just got divorced because it wasn't working out. Her mom spends a good deal of time with her, but she is also reaching out to female friends where she can vent her hurt and anger about men. When Vickie asks Mom why she and Dad got divorced, her mom tells her that it didn't work out, that she learned some unhealthy things about relationships when she was growing up, and that she is learning to deal with it through the support of friends and a therapy group. She tells Vickie that not all men are bad and that she had a part in it too. And then she says that that's all there is to it. They go on and talk about something else, and then Vickie goes out with her friends and has a good time, trusting that Mom is handling her own pain in a good way.

Addicted Parents:

John's parents were both addicted to cocaine. John is eight. His parents both went to treatment for their addiction and are now actively involved in 12-Step groups and recovery work around their childhoods. They talk to John a lot about the evils of chemicals. They share many details about how they were hurt and abused in childhood. Sometimes John gets bored. Sometimes he gets scared. Sometimes he gets angry. And he is getting very enmeshed in their lives.

Al is nine. His parents have both been to treatment for alcoholism. They sat him down one day and said, "We became addicted to alcohol. We now go to meetings to help us stay sober. We know that life around here was not good for you. We will be going to some family therapy to help all of us talk about this. But you need to know this is *our* problem, not yours. We will not drown you in information about recovery. You can go about your life, and we will stay sober."

Al feels a lot better, is beginning to trust his parents again and has his own life.

About Parents' Sex Lives:

Carol is 16. Her mom tells her how frustrated she is with her dad because he doesn't satisfy her sexually. Carol is very concerned, tries to listen, tries to make suggestions and is getting overwhelmed. Part of her is very worried, part of her wonders if her sex life will be awful when she grows up and part of her is titillated by all of Mom's sexual talk.

Betty is also 16. Her dad and mom are having some sexual problems. They chose to talk about it with an expert in sexual therapy. They haven't said a word about it to Betty, because they know that it's not her problem and that it would be abusive to do so.

Should We Cry In Front Of Our Kids?

Of course we should. It's how we do it that counts. Being out of control, letting our children sit in the middle of our grief and begin to carry it for us is not okay. Feelings that are out of control, that are exaggerated because of an untreated addiction, that are scary and overwhelming, should be dealt with in therapy. Likewise, the majority of our grief, the very deep grief, needs to be shared with other adults in most cases.

The setting is important, too. At a funeral, where crying is socially supported and where many people are doing it, is safe, even if it is deep grieving. Crying with our kids during the first few days or weeks after a catastrophic loss gives them permission to cry, too. The trick is to have our tears, but not overwhelm with them. To cry, but not draw our children into being our source of comfort during our grief.

Money Talk:

How much should our kids know about our finances? Families vary on this one. In the case where we are in financial trouble and experiencing a lot of stress, it is important to tell the kids that we are going to have to tighten our belts, but that it is not the kids' problem and we will make it somehow. Kids should not be dragged into money worries. The adults in the system are supposed to handle the finances and give information to the kids as it is needed. For example, if things are tight this year, it would be appropriate to say, "Kids, we aren't going to have as much money as we did last year. We will need to cut back on our spending, which means we will have to do without some of the things we normally bought last year."

Cancer:

When Dad or Mom finds out that they have a serious illness or even a terminal illness, it is very important to sit down, have a family meeting, share feelings about it and as with all the other issues above, stay in charge. There are subtle cues we give off that either let kids have the information and then their feelings, or that let kids have the information and then get overwhelmed. We need to be realistic about the illness. Let kids know the basics about the treatment and what will happen during treatment. Let them know that it's scary, but that you have the resources to deal with that fear and get support from adults. Let them ask questions, even if they ask if you may die. Be honest without being manipulative. And if the illness is terminal, at some point it is essential for you to face that, and *then* help your family face it. We have seen some *amazing* healing take place in families as they face the death of one of their members. Family therapy during a crisis like this can leave the family healthier and clearer than ever before, which is the greatest gift we can leave our loved ones.

54

When My Teenager Is Going To Have A Baby

Ah, parenthood! They say it is filled with joys and with sorrows, which is very true. Life is filled with joys and sorrows as well. We would all do a bit better if we could remind ourselves of this fact now and then. Nobody *ever* said we had to be perfect or do the job of raising children perfectly. Nobody!

So what do we do when our son or daughter, age 15, nervous, on the verge of tears, terrified, excited, shame-filled, angry, lonely, hurt, mortified, shaking, nauseous, frightened and confused comes to us and announces that he or she will become a parent in seven and a half months?

- Some dysfunctional parents get really angry right away. Their anger is most often about their own fear of sexuality, about their inability to let go of their children who are rapidly growing up, about their shame and embarrassment because they believe that whatever their nearly grown children do is about themselves instead of about their nearly grown children. Getting angry right away is a great strategy if you want to be hated by your children and if you want your children to remain confused and dependent on you forever. Hmmm. Maybe that's why you're doing it.

231

- Some dysfunctional parents want to rush in and do lots of fixing right away. "Well," they say supportively, "I think the first thing you need to do is run right down to the doctor to see if you should be on any vitamins or anything. Then you ought to go talk to Sally Jones, the psychologist. She can help you decide what you need to do. You look a little tired, dear. Do you want to go up and take a little nap before dinner? Here, let me get you a blanket." Etc. Wanting to do and fix and come up with solutions and answers right away is a great way to stay away from feelings, isn't it? It's called problem-solving but in affairs of the heart, it is really *problem-causing*.

What then should we say? We recommend you sit down with your teenager, holding his or her hand if it seems appropriate. Let there be plenty of silence in the air if need be. Put your own beliefs and feelings aside, *completely* aside. Create an environment of *total emotional safety* for your teenager. All else will flow from there. You can ask how they *feel*. If they're scared and don't talk right away, don't start blabbering or asking questions — let the silence be there until your child/adult is ready to talk to you. Concentrate on feelings. When they *do* talk, validate what you hear.

Say things like, "Yeah, that sounds really scary" and "I'd be really confused, too" and "You can take your time and have your feelings. You don't have to make any decisions right away."

It's amazing what almost any teenager will come up with on their own if we just validate and support. Teenagers are quite often able to do all the problem-solving part of it themselves; and if they aren't, they'll *ask us* for help if we have created that *emotional safety* mentioned above.

Did you think we were going to write a whole book on this topic? Surprise! If you can do just half of what we have mentioned here, you'll be well on your way to great success with your teenagers.

55

Those In-Laws!

You can pick your friends, but you can't pick your relatives. That's pretty sage observing, we must say. What *do* we do with our relatives? How much time with them is enough? What if they are abusive? What if one of us likes them and the other one doesn't? Here are *some* of the answers that we have seen work out.

- Some people really like their relatives and spend quite a bit of time with them. They have other friends outside of the family system, and they do a lot with them, too.
- Some people have very abusive parents and relatives who are unrecovering alcoholics, offenders and even child molesters. It is very important to stay away from ongoing abuse. We have recommended to all but a few in these cases to keep the door to the family open by sending a Christmas card and perhaps birthday cards. There is always the chance that even in the most abusive families someone will eventually decide to get help. But don't threaten your own safety and health by subjecting yourself to constant abuse.

- Some people have parents and relatives who are somewhere in between these extremes. Learn to measure your tolerance for the dysfunction in the family. The family may expect you, your spouse and children to spend all weekends and holidays at The Family Compound. You don't have to do this. In fact, it is not possible to do this and then spend time with relatives on the other side of the family. Spending all of your free time with family isn't healthy, either. We are supposed to go out into the world when we grow up and create new systems with friends and hobbies and the like which doesn't leave room to spend every weekend with relatives.
- It is okay for one of you to visit relatives while the other does something with friends. If your relatives think that this is a sign that your relationship is in trouble, just calmly reply that the relationship is not in trouble.
- It is okay for one of you to like Uncle Joe while the other one does not. But only if you do not let this difference drive a wedge between you. If this starts to happen, look deeper to see why you both believe that you have to agree on everything.
- If your children are being used or abused by relatives, you always have the *duty* to intervene and take whatever steps are necessary to prevent the abuse from happening in the future, even if this means not letting the children be around the relatives. Be careful here, too. Sometimes we project our own stuff into these situations. Sometimes our kids are treated okay by relatives even though we weren't when we were little.
- Ask yourself if battling over in-laws is worth the end of your own relationship. Learn to let go of childhood expectations. Realize that your partner may have different needs than you. Stick together and support each other on these touchy questions.

56

What To Expect
When Our Parents
Grow Old

What to do with aging parents, how to treat them and how to protect ourselves from the abuse of our aging parents is the most difficult problem many of us will ever face in our lives. As our parents grow old and approach death, powerful forces inside of us come to the fore. Co-dependent and self-abusive behaviors that we thought we had overcome suddenly return. Guilt, shame, fear and feelings of abandonment surface. An urge to complete unfinished business becomes overwhelming for many of us. It can be an extremely painful time.

In very functional families, the problem of aging parents is also difficult. Our lifestyles have changed so much in the past 30 years that there are barely any ground rules for how to handle our older parents. Do we put them in a nursing home because both of us work and there would be no one at home to care for them? Does one of us quit our job, leaving us with the possibility of severe financial stress? How often do we visit our parents? How do we confront them gently when they are not able to handle their own affairs? All of these questions face people in the 1990s and beyond.

If you came from a dysfunctional family, it makes it that much harder. And if the rest of the family, parents included, have done little in the way of growth and recovery, it makes it intolerably painful. We want our family to heal. And we want our parents to heal before they die. We don't want to bury them while we still have deep anger and hurt from the past.

Each of us must find our own way through this maze of feelings and beliefs and confusion. What we have found is that there are as many ways to deal with aging parents as there are human beings on earth. Some people have to play it out in all its agony, staying dysfunctionally connected and abused by their parents right to the end. Only then can they begin to break free of those terrible bonds of victimization. Other people get tons of support and help to break those bonds before their parents die. They stay involved, but in much healthier ways — keeping their distance when the abuse is at its worst and approaching carefully when it is not.

If The Family Is Healthy . . .

In functional families certain things happen during this time that do not happen in unhealthy families. Functional families:

1. Share the work, the time, the money and the effort in caring for aging parents.
2. The parents who are growing old have a lot of peace and serenity and are not afraid of death, and so much of the crabbiness, irritability and abuse is absent. Or it is completely gone.
3. When brain deterioration occurs, as in Alzheimer's disease, healthy families make the tough decisions that have to be made, such as providing institutional care, but they do so lovingly and respectfully; and then they grieve openly and share the emotional burden.
4. Healthy families seek help openly when they need it.
5. People in healthy families respect the wisdom of old age and include older people in family functions where possible.
6. They talk about death. They let the older person process the past.

7. They are open to healing old wounds through talking and by feeling. They can forgive after holding each other accountable.

8. They see their parents' dignified death as a sign of hope rather than as a beacon of despair. They understand what Erik Erikson meant when he wrote:

Healthy children will not fear life if their elders have integrity enough not to fear death.

If The Family Is Unhealthy . . .

If the family is still quite dysfunctional, the imminent death of either parent will trigger a wellspring of acting out, re-enactments of earlier abuses and tons of stress and confusion. Adult children who are still enmeshed with the parent will try desperately to maintain their "special" bond with that parent, even if it is an abusive one. Children who never got enough from that parent will try to get it now, often with little reward, or they will stay so removed from the parent that they feel terrible guilt after the parent dies. Siblings who grew to hate each other because of the unfair treatment they received by their parents will rekindle those flames of hatred. And clear feelings of resolution will rarely emerge.

In very dysfunctional families, it is especially important for Recovering Adult Children to . . .

1. Maintain your sobriety and recovery no matter what.
2. Stay deeply connected to your support system and yell for professional help before you succumb to the urges of drowning with the rest of the family.
3. If possible, maintain contact with the aging/dying parent, but change the rules. Leave when abuse begins, stating that you will return when it stops.
4. Don't get manipulated into doing all of the work. In many families, one sibling gets the major responsibility for taking care of the parents.

5. *Expect* to *not* get all you would like in terms of healing, resolution of feelings and closure with the dying parent. A friend of ours whose father was dying kept her distance, but also stayed present during her father's painful death. She visited the hospital but left when it became abusive. Her father had never told her that he loved her and deep down inside she was hoping that he would tell her. Only minutes before he died, he came back into consciousness, raised up from his bed, threw his arms around her and said, "I love you." It was a tremendously moving moment. She grieved his death and shared her feelings with her friends and healthier loved ones.

And then suddenly one night, about a week after the funeral, she bolted up in bed one night and exclaimed clearly and forcefully to her husband, "Damn, I'm so damned mad! Why in the *hell* did he have to wait until he was on his deathbed? It's not enough! It just isn't enough." It was the healthiest thing she had ever done in her life. She took what was given, but refused to diminish herself by pretending that she had received what she needed from her father. From that point on she was able to live her life as a free and healthy adult.

6. Expect to feel guilty, sad, shameful, angry, hurt and con-fused after your parent dies. There will be many feelings to resolve and much pain to heal. If you expect it, it won't surprise you or make you feel defective. Then you can get on with the very important business of healing and living a functional life.

57

The Bear:
Continued

The Big Brown Bear and his mate traveled long and far after his foot had been sorely damaged in the bear trap. It was physically very painful for him to walk, and for both of them it was emotionally painful to leave their part of the woods. After days and days of walking, they finally came to rest along the banks of a new stream. There they settled down to have their family. Months later, his mate gave birth to two cubs. As the cubs nursed at their mother's breast, the Big Brown Bear hunted for food and watched constantly for danger. His mate was sometimes so frightened by the memories of the bear trap that she would not produce enough milk for her cubs. They lay awake at night, obsessed with the possibility of danger. The cubs were beginning to feel the anxiety themselves as their hearts beat fast and they slept fitfully. Their lives had become a continual nightmare, in which they were all entrapped.

Finally one day, as he was ambling down to the stream to drink some clear, icy water and look for a stray salmon or two, he smelled something odd. It was the scent of an animal, but not of one he had ever smelled before. His heart quickened and he scampered behind some thick brush near the water. Then he spotted the animal off in the distance. It stood erect, and it had very little body hair. Dangling from one of its arms was something familiar. His spine shuddered and the horrible memories of agonizing hours caught in the trap flashed before his eyes. The blood, the pain, the terror and the sadness of what he thought was the end of his life with his mate all came into view again! And then, from the fog of his memories and of his tiny brain, a flash of insight swept through him.

The Big Brown Bear waited and watched. The man carrying the bear trap approached the stream, looked around for bear tracks, and then walked a few feet back into the woods, out of sight. A few moments later, he emerged from the woods again, crossed the stream and walked away. The Big Brown Bear moved toward that place in the woods where the man had just been. He moved very carefully this time, and he watched the ground with care before putting his foot down with each step. A few moments later, he saw the bear trap — cold, ugly, rusty jaws open and waiting for him to die. He shuddered again. The trap was now just within inches of his curious nose. A fury came over him that he had never experienced before. A rage so powerful that he did not know if he could contain himself. And then, just before he crashed his paw down on top of the awful trap, he stopped, turned, and with a sweep of his huge foot, he smashed a large tree branch into the center of the trap. He heard a frightening **whack!** It was exactly the same sound he had heard many months ago. He looked at the trap and knew that it had been disarmed.

A few hours later, the Big Brown Bear entered their den with two fresh salmon in his mouth for his family. His mate immediately sensed that something was different. He radiated peacefulness. He looked as if he had been reborn. He didn't even limp as noticeably as he had done before. His cubs sensed this change, too, and they leaped toward him playfully, trying to wrestle him to the ground. His mate began to cry tears of relief and joy.

Years later, as the Big Brown Bear and his mate sat by the edge of their stream and watched their grandchildren romp in the forest, the memories of that tragic day when he got caught in the trap were still clear, but very faint. They had long since stopped being consumed by those memories. The Big Brown Bear had taught his cubs how to smell the presence of man, and he had taught them how to disarm those ugly traps before they stepped into them. The Big Brown Bear and his mate nuzzled each other affectionately, secure that what they had learned would be passed down to all of their heirs, and that they could die in peace.

PART VIII

Moving On
Into Life

Life is a series of surprises.

Ralph Waldo Emerson
Circles, 1841

58

There *Is*
No Failure

As you use this book, please remember that there *is no failure* in life. Life is really a series of starts and stops as we try to become the person we were meant to be. Many of us get sidetracked by the childhood abuse and neglect we experienced, but we are all on the same grand course. We believe that until you breathe your last breath, you always have a chance to try something new — to actualize yet another part of yourself.

Remember that each new thing we try teaches us something, and that being functional means we are open to learning from both our successes *and* our failures. If we cannot learn from our mistakes, we cannot go forward. If we cannot *make* mistakes, we will always be going backwards.

Try out some of the things in this book. One or two of them might just work for you.

Other Books By . . .
Health Communications

ADULT CHILDREN OF ALCOHOLICS
Janet Woititz
Over a year on *The New York Times* Best-Seller list, this book is the primer on Adult Children of Alcoholics.
ISBN 0-932194-15-X $6.95

STRUGGLE FOR INTIMACY
Janet Woititz
Another best-seller, this book gives insightful advice on learning to love more fully.
ISBN 0-932194-25-7 $6.95

BRADSHAW ON: THE FAMILY: A Revolutionary Way of Self-Discovery
John Bradshaw
The host of the nationally televised series of the same name shows us how families can be healed and individuals can realize full potential.
ISBN 0-932194-54-0 $9.95

HEALING THE SHAME THAT BINDS YOU
John Bradshaw
This important book shows how toxic shame is the core problem in our compulsions and offers new techniques of recovery vital to all of us.
ISBN 0-932194-86-9 $9.95

HEALING THE CHILD WITHIN: Discovery and Recovery for
Adult Children of Dysfunctional Families — Charles Whitfield, M.D.
Dr. Whitfield defines, describes and discovers how we can reach our Child Within to heal and nurture our woundedness.
ISBN 0-932194-40-0 $8.95

A GIFT TO MYSELF: A Personal Guide To Healing My Child Within
Charles L. Whitfield, M.D.
Dr. Whitfield provides practical guidelines and methods to work through the pain and confusion of being an Adult Child of a dysfunctional family.
ISBN 1-55874-042-2 $11.95

HEALING TOGETHER: A Guide To Intimacy And Recovery For
Co-dependent Couples — Wayne Kritsberg, M.A.
This is a practical book that tells the reader why he or she gets into dysfunctional and painful relationships, and then gives a concrete course of action on how to move the relationship toward health.
ISBN 1-55784-053-8 $8.95

3201 S.W. 15th Street,
Deerfield Beach, FL 33442
1-800-851-9100

Health
Communications, Inc.

Books from . . .
Health Communications

PERFECT DAUGHTERS: Adult Daughters Of Alcoholics
Robert Ackerman
Through a combined narrative of professional and anecdotal styles Robert
Ackerman helps restore a sense of balance in life for Adult Daughters of
Alcoholics.
ISBN 1-55874-040-6 $8.95

I DON'T WANT TO BE ALONE:
For Men And Women Who Want To Heal Addictive Relationships
John Lee
John Lee describes the problems of co-dependent relationships and his
realization that he may be staying in such a relationship because of his
fear of being alone.
ISBN 1-55874-065-1 $8.95

SHAME AND GUILT: Masters Of Disguise
Jane Middelton-Moz
The author uses myths and fairy tales to portray different shaming
environments and to show how shame can keep you from being the
person you were born to be.
ISBN 1-55874-072-4 $8.95

LIFESKILLS FOR ADULT CHILDREN
Janet G. Woititz and Alan Garner
This book teaches you the interpersonal skills that can make your life easier
while improving your sense of self-worth. Examples are provided to help
clarify the lessons and exercises are given for practicing your new skills.
ISBN 1-55874-070-8 $8.95

THE MIRACLE OF RECOVERY:
Healing For Addicts, Adult Children And Co-dependents
Sharon Wegscheider-Cruse
This is about the good news — that recovery from co-dependency is
possible. Sharon offers ways to embrace the positive aspects of one's
experience — to realize the strength that can come from adversity.
Celebrate your own miracle with this inspiring book.
ISBN 1-55874-024-4 $9.95

SHIPPING/HANDLING: All orders shipped UPS unless weight exceeds 200 lbs., special routing is requested, or
delivery territory is outside continental U.S. Orders outside United States shipped either Air Parcel Post or Surface
Parcel Post. Shipping and handling charges apply to all orders shipped whether UPS, Book Rate, Library Rate, Air
or Surface Parcel Post or Common Carrier and will be charged as follows. Orders less than $25.00 in value add
$2.00 minimum. Orders from $25.00 to $50.00 in value (after discount) add $2.50 minimum. Orders greater than
$50.00 in value (after discount) add 6% of value. Orders greater than $25.00 outside United States add 15% of
value. We are not responsible for loss or damage unless material is shipped UPS. Allow 3-5 weeks after receipt of
order for delivery. Prices are subject to change without prior notice.

3201 S.W. 15th Street,
Deerfield Beach, FL 33442-8124
1-800-851-9100

Health Communications, Inc.

Helpful 12-Step Books from . . .
Health Communications

12 STEPS TO SELF-PARENTING For Adult Children
Philip Oliver-Diaz, M.S.W., and Patricia A. O'Gorman, Ph.D.
This gentle 12-Step guide takes the reader from pain to healing and self-parenting, from anger to forgiveness, and from fear and despair to recovery.
ISBN 0-932194-68-0 $7.95

SELF-PARENTING 12-STEP WORKBOOK: Windows To Your Inner Child
Patricia O'Gorman, Ph.D., and Philip Oliver-Diaz, M.S.W.
This workbook invites you to become the complete individual you were born to be by using visualizations, exercises and experiences designed to reconnect you to your inner child.
ISBN 1-55874-052-X $9.95

THE 12-STEP STORY BOOKLETS
Mary M. McKee
Each beautifully illustrated booklet deals with a step, using a story from nature in parable form. The 12 booklets (one for each step) lead us to a better understanding of ourselves and our recovery.
ISBN 1-55874-002-3 $8.95

VIOLENT VOICES:
12 Steps To Freedom From Emotional And Verbal Abuse
Kay Porterfield, M.A.
By using the healing model of the 12 Steps emotionally abused women are shown how to deal effectively with verbal and psychological abuse and to begin living as healed and whole people.
ISBN 1-55874-028-7 $9.95

GIFTS FOR PERSONAL GROWTH & RECOVERY
Wayne Kritsberg
A goldmine of positive techniques for recovery (affirmations, journal writing, visualizations, guided meditations, etc.), this book is indispensable for those seeking personal growth.
ISBN 0-932194-60-5 $6.95

3201 S.W. 15th Street,
Deerfield Beach, FL 33442-8124
1-800-851-9100

Health
Communications, Inc.